BASICS
FASHION DESIGN
08

STYLING

Ethical: aware-
ness/
reflect-
ion/
debate

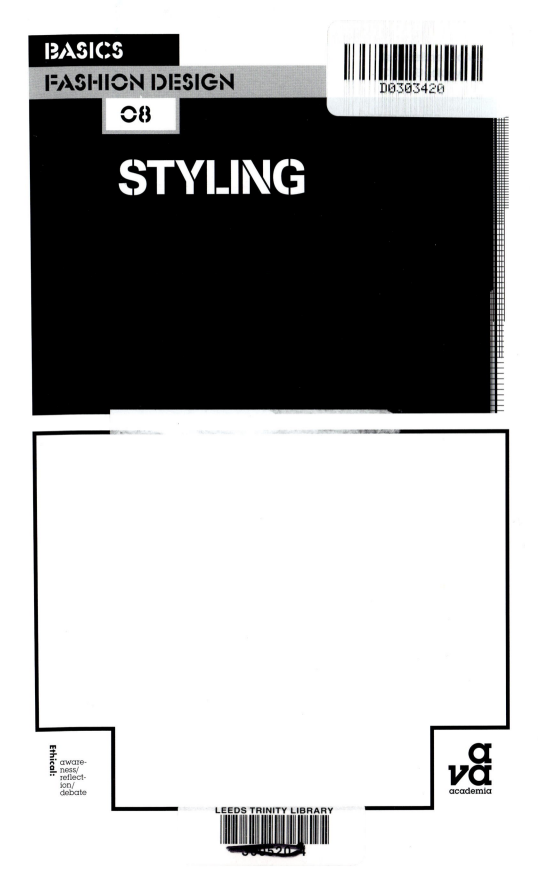

a
va
academia

An AVA Book

Published by AVA Publishing SA
Rue des Fontenailles 16
Case Postale
1000 Lausanne 6
Switzerland
Tel: +41 786 005 109
Email: enquiries@avabooks.com

Distributed by Thames & Hudson (ex-North America)
181a High Holborn
London WC1V 7QX
United Kingdom
Tel: +44 20 7845 5000
Fax: +44 20 7845 5055
Email: sales@thameshudson.co.uk
www.thamesandhudson.com

Distributed in the USA & Canada by:
Ingram Publisher Services Inc.
1 Ingram Blvd.
La Vergne TN 37086
USA
Tel: +1 866 400 5351
Fax: +1 800 838 1149
Email: customer.service@ingrampublisherservices.com

English Language Support Office
AVA Publishing (UK) Ltd.
Tel: +44 1903 204 455
Email: enquiries@avabooks.com

ISBN 978-2-940411-39-9

Library of Congress Cataloging-in-Publication Data
Buckley, Clare; McAssey, Jacqueline.
Basics Fashion Design 08: Styling /
Clare Buckley, Jacqueline McAssey p. cm.
Includes bibliographical references and index.
ISBN: 9782940411399 (pbk.:alk.paper)
eISBN: 9782940447138
1.Fashion design--Study and teaching.2.Design--Study and teaching.
TT580 .B835 2011

10 9 8 7 6 5 4 3 2 1

Design by Pseudonym

Production by AVA Book Production Pte. Ltd., Singapore
Tel: +65 6334 8173
Fax: +65 6259 9830
Email: production@avabooks.com.sg

○ **Menswear editorial entitled
'Apocalypse Joyeuse'.**
Photography: Adrian Meško
Styling: Ryan Lobo

Contents

Put simply, a fashion stylist is responsible for choosing the look and clothing, and often much more, to communicate a fashion idea, trend or theme, or to advertise a fashion product. This book has been written for those who are interested in the process of fashion image making and what the job entails. It will inform you about how and why the stylist has become an integral part of fashion image making in magazines, newspapers and advertising campaigns, and more recently as a consultant to fashion designers and brands.

You will also learn what it means, for example, to style for a catalogue, a still-life image or a fashion show and what types of skills these different fields require. Personal styling is explained in its various guises, from one-to-one styling in retail outlets to the styling of musicians and celebrities. Additionally, it will describe the day-to-day life of a stylist, which should help you to identify if this is the right career choice for you.

This book contains visual examples of inspirational styling, created not only by professionals but also undergraduates; proving that even on a limited budget, with imagination and drive, it is still possible to create beautiful and relevant work.

◗ 'Let's do it all over the world', a fashion editorial for *V Magazine*.
Photography: Will Davidson
Styling: Jay Massacret

○ **Muted menswear is shot against a dramatic landscape in this fashion editorial for *V Man*.**
Photography: Will Davidson
Styling: Mattias Karlsson

Essentially, styling is a way of assembling clothing and accessories, to exhibit them in their most desirable or attractive way in order to sell them. This could include, for example, choosing accessories (belt, shoes and jewellery) to coordinate with and complement a dress. Fashion clothing can be styled alone or as a group of products (showing a range of colours); with or without a model. The styling process involves selecting and experimenting with many alternative garments to establish the perfect composition.

'I wanted to mix designer things with "found" things, and used to go to places like John Lewis' schoolboys' department to get a very eclectic mix.'
Melanie Ward

The origins of styling

The first stylists were fashion editors who worked exclusively for fashion magazines. Editors did in fact 'edit' the clothing and fashion pages, and they chose the designers to be featured in the magazine. Under the initial direction of the fashion editor the relationship that really mattered during the shoot was that of the photographer and model. Indeed, during the 1960s it was common for models to do their own make-up and hair and bring their own accessories to a shoot, foregoing the need for a third person. Then, during the 1980s the first freelance stylists appeared, working for new style magazines such as *The Face* and *i-D*. As these magazines did not have permanent fashion staff, freelance stylists could apply their inventive fashion ideas across a number of publications and clients. The stylist became an integral part of fashion editorial; a key contributor to the image-making process, who wasn't tied to one magazine or one point of view.

◖ **Fashion editorial for *V Magazine* where the couple's monochrome attire is coordinated.**
Photography: Will Davidson
Styling: Jay Massacret

What is fashion styling? > Aspects of the job

Roles in styling

Stylists work in fashion editorial styling (magazines and newspapers); commercial fashion styling (advertising); in fashion shows and events; and as personal stylists for individual clients. The stylist's moniker also varies: they may be known as wardrobe stylists; on a magazine or newspaper they are called fashion editors and assistants and in fashion stores they can be referred to as personal shoppers.

Aside from the practical nature of the subject, styling is very much the opinion of the stylist, who imparts their often intuitive view on fashion. Even as a new stylist you are not judged on your practical skills alone; your own ideas, vision and taste are evident in each piece of work you produce.

Challenging perceptions

Styling can also challenge perceptions of fashion and style to move clothing in a new direction and pieces can be put together in a way not originally intended by the designer. Fashion history is littered with these examples, which now seem commonplace: underwear worn as outerwear; women in men's formal attire; sports apparel placed in a fashion environment. Whether carefully coordinated or artfully juxtaposed, both approaches have their place in fashion styling.

◐ Styling with colour, words and props.
Photography: Alex Hurst
Styling: Jacqueline McAssey

◐ Fashion turned on its head.
Photography: Marcus Palmqvist
Styling: Ellen Af Geijerstam

What is fashion styling? > Aspects of the job

Ray Petri (1948–1989)

Ray Petri, thought by many to be the first stylist, was known in the 1980s for his 'Buffalo' style; a groundbreaking mix of urban uniform, ethnic dress, sportswear and high-end fashion. His use of real people in fashion shoots instead of models (including black and mixed-race men) was, at the time, new and exciting. Petri contributed to *The Face* magazine and worked with designers Jean Paul Gaultier and Giorgio Armani. The creative collective he was part of was also named Buffalo and in the book of the same name, *GQ* editor Dylan Jones stated that even 20 years after Petri's death, 'Harder than the rest; in the age of the stylist, Ray Petri is still king.'

❍ Buffalo-style fashion editorial combining sportswear and a Chris Ofili-inspired print.
Photography and styling: Danielle Smith, Sally Pickering and Bridie McCann

❍ Fashion editorial inspired by the style of Neneh Cherry.
Photography: Si Miller
Styling: Eve Fenlon

The nature of a stylist's job is very much dependent on the specific field in which they work. Some stylists will stick to one field throughout their career whilst others will move easily between the various forms of styling; some will work permanently for one magazine, company or studio, others work in a freelance capacity. The stylist's overall input to a project can also vary considerably. A stylist working for a magazine or newspaper may have a responsibility to create something in line with a particular aesthetic and as such will have more control of a project; whereas a stylist working on an advertising campaign is likely to be part of a large team and will defer to the client and the brief. These different working methods are further explained in Chapter 3.

Along with the photographer, the stylist is a key member of the photoshoot crew and the planning and production of the shoot is often well within the stylist's remit. They may source appropriate locations, attend model castings and direct the shoot brief, as well as look after the model on the shoot day itself and generally ensure that proceedings go smoothly. What follows is a basic explanation of what is expected of a stylist working in the fashion industry today.

Fashion editorial influenced by fetish clothing and the 1967 film *Belle de Jour*.
Photography and styling: Ellie Noble

Fashion research

As a fashion stylist you are expected to keep up with everything fashion related, including determining trends in fashion. Editorial stylists view the seasonal collections that are presented at the fashion weeks in New York, London, Milan and Paris. They will analyze the collections, recording details such as key silhouettes, colours, prints and textures, and use this information to determine the key clothing trends they think will inspire their readers. Trend information is translated differently from publication to publication into fashion stories. When developing the story idea, the stylist needs to take into account the content and tone of the story, the model, type of shoot location and price of clothing according to the type of publication and its readership.

Stylists working on commercial projects should have a good awareness of the brand and the consumer. An advertising job will usually have a strict brief so a good commercial stylist will be able to follow it to the letter. Once the fashion story or advertising brief has been discussed and developed by the creative team, it is the stylist's job to work out how to achieve it.

In addition, stylists should be undertaking other research methods to inform their work; this could be anything from visiting art exhibitions and looking at street style imagery online to travelling and exploring other cities and cultures. See Chapter 2 for more on research.

O Louis Vuitton S/S11. Conducting research is important for all stylists, as is being able to critically analyze the seasonal collections.
Catwalking.com

Sourcing

Stylists are responsible for sourcing the clothes, accessories and often the props for a shoot. This mainly involves contacting the PR agencies and clothing brands and 'calling in' clothes for specific shoot dates and times. The clothing may be viewed online, in designers' lookbooks or by visiting PR showrooms after fashion week. It is often a competitive business: there may be only a few samples of any one style; if a piece isn't available the stylist may receive an alternative choice (or nothing!).

Stylists will also source vintage or period clothing from specialist outlets or collectors, or access historical clothing from costumiers. Stylists often make it their business to find up-and-coming designers, which gives them access to new and exciting fashion. There are no rules on how materials are sourced; they only have to be appropriate to the project.

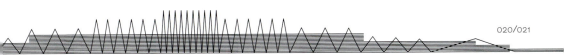

Models

Liaising with model agencies is an important part of a stylist's job. The stylist and the photographer will look at the models available in different agencies, shortlist a number who may be right for the shoot, and the stylist will then check availability. The magazine or client normally has the final approval regarding the model, who is central to any editorial or commercial story.

What is fashion styling? > **Aspects of the job** > A career in fashion styling

Clothing

From the moment clothes are in your possession the designer, PR or retailer expects you to look after them. This means protecting clothes both in storage and during transit to shoots; ensuring that they are not soiled with make-up, and that they don't go missing from a set – essentially, returning them in the same condition as they came. Any clothing used in a shoot must be thoroughly documented with the designer or brand name, description and price. This is vital for editorial styling because readers need to know the cost and stockist information for any featured clothing.

◓ **Example of a fashion rail, showing source details attached to each garment.**

◓ **Example of a stylist's portfolio.**
Styling: Kate Geaney

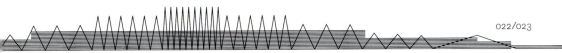
Your portfolio

Building and maintaining an up-to-date portfolio is essential for gaining more styling work; it should contain the very best examples of your work. When a photoshoot ends and the editing or retouching has been done the photographer will normally supply the stylist with final images for their portfolio. For editorial work, magazine tears can be presented in a portfolio in addition to photographs.

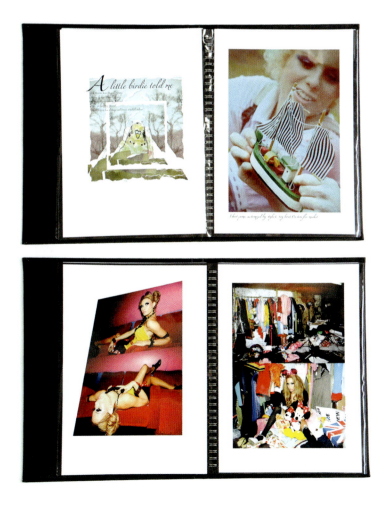

Aspects of the job

Freelance

Working as a freelance stylist can be challenging, with the risk of irregular work, job cancellations, no fixed income and no holiday or sick pay. On the plus side, working in a freelance capacity offers the opportunity to meet new people, to work on different projects day to day and to travel more. Good stylists may want to be represented by an agent who will find work on their behalf and send out their portfolio to prospective clients. For every job the agent procures they will take a portion of the stylist's fee.

Administration

Styling involves a great deal of paperwork: keeping a record of clothes that have been borrowed; proof of how and when the clothes were despatched, whether by courier or by hand. For freelance stylists the paperwork increases dramatically; they also have to provide evidence of expenditure (such as receipts from styling jobs) and invoices for tax reasons.

○ **Backstage at Louise Goldin A/W10 (left) and Graeme Black A/W09 (right).**
Photography: Justine Grist

Lifestyle

What people don't often realize is just how physically demanding the stylist's job can be. It requires lots of energy to pull heavy bags of clothes, rails or steamers from car to studio and back again. The stylist is present during the set-up of a shoot and is always last one to leave, making sure the location has been left immaculately clean. Such a demanding schedule can affect one's home and social life.

Consultancy

Today's stylists are taking on increasingly sophisticated roles. Some have close relationships with fashion designers, playing a part in influencing the design process and presentation of collections. As creative directors they use their unique research skills and knowledge to inspire new fashion collections and direct fashion shows. The level of experience required for consultancy is generally attained over a number of years of working at a professional level.

The traditional route of a fashion stylist was through journalism, with the fashion editor reporting on trends and creating fashion stories using words and visuals. However, there are now many established stylists who have entered the profession by studying fashion design and other creative disciplines; there are some who have not studied fashion at all. There are no hard and fast rules to beginning your styling career. There are benefits in both assisting a stylist and taking a course in styling, and in this section you will find arguments for both approaches. Transferable skills are also vital to the job of a stylist. Knowing how to organize your time, communicate with other people, work as part of a team and solve problems are all key to your professional and personal development.

'The editor of French *Vogue*, Carine Roitfeld, began life not as a wordsmith or manager but as a stylist.'
Tamsin Blanchard

○ **Fashion editorial for** ***Harper's Bazaar* magazine.**
Photography: Jonas Bresnan
Styling: Vanessa Coyle

The fashion stylist

A career in fashion styling

Assisting a stylist

One route into styling is as an assistant,
either for a professional stylist or at a
magazine or newspaper. Learning the trade
in this manner is an excellent way to be
trained on the job, which will make you more
independent. Assisting enables you to pick
up practical skills and tips while you work and
possibly receive payment for your
endeavours. You will meet other creative
people who may help with your career and
there may be opportunities to travel. What is
more, if you then decide to embark on a
fashion or styling college course, you will
almost certainly start as an assistant
upon graduation.

First of all you will have to find someone to assist or someone who will give you experience and, as this is a competitive field, you may find this the most difficult part. You will be in competition with hundreds of college students who are also looking for styling experience, but who may have portfolios or examples of work they have already produced. If you are lucky enough to find a freelance stylist to assist, their work pattern is likely to be erratic and, essentially, you will work when they have work. They may have periods where they work constantly (including weekends or at nights) and other times that are not so busy. As an assistant, payment for your work can be intermittent or nonexistent. When you start out, you will usually be working not for the money, but because you love what you do.

Your individual approach in implementing what you have learnt, your networking skills and, crucially, an element of luck, will all determine how successful you are in any creative industry. Networking is important but it doesn't mean speaking only to those you consider important. You can meet like-minded people anywhere: at exhibitions, fashion shows or parties. Be approachable. Listen to what people have to say about themselves and their work. Along with your talent you will be remembered and re-employed based on how you work with and treat other people.

Fashion education

Opting for a fashion education is for many the first step into the industry. Imagery is at the heart of most fashion courses, many of which offer fashion styling as part of the curriculum. Styling can be taught as a single subject or, to a lesser degree, as part of another field such as design or marketing. If you decide that studying a course in styling is the best route for you, then you must do your research. As well as covering subject-specific and key skills, most styling-related courses offer theoretical studies, such as marketing and business or cultural and contextual essays.

The benefits of a fashion education are evident. Higher education encourages you to undertake more in-depth research; to experiment and test ideas. In addition, you have a ready supply of specialist equipment and the space in which to carry out your work. More importantly, you have opportunities for cross-course collaborative projects with your peers, such as photography, design or illustration, for example. A good fashion course will also develop your employability skills by bringing in industry speakers and setting up industry-related projects, which give you insight into styling in the real world.

◖ ◗ **Fashion editorial entitled** *Deuil Aveu,* **which means 'mourning confession'.**
Photography: Jemma Rylah
Styling: Chloë Amer

Fashion styling

Studying styling as your major subject allows you to explore it in greater depth, learn practical techniques and even specialize in an area of styling, such as editorial or commercial. Some courses teach make-up as a complementary subject for those students who are interested in both.

Fashion design

Learning to design and make fashion garments and collections are valuable skills to a fashion stylist. Design graduates have knowledge of garment construction and how clothing fits the body; they can handle fabric well and have good sewing techniques. As a stylist, this means you will be able to style your own work for photoshoots.

Aspects of the job > **A career in fashion styling** > Interview: Christopher Shannon

Fashion journalism

If you want to write articles and features, conduct interviews and style fashion for print, the Internet (websites and blogs) or for broadcast, such as TV or film, then this route is best for you. You will need very good writing skills to gain a place on this type of course.

Fashion communication, imaging, promotion and marketing

Course content varies significantly by institution but generally speaking, these courses teach you how to visually and verbally communicate ideas through, for example, the production of a magazine concept or the promotion of a product or service. Usually these courses teach commercial and editorial styling alongside other subjects such as PR, graphic design, trend forecasting, visual merchandising and so on; they are good if you want an overview of fashion without having to focus on the design of clothing.

BANANAMAN

MARC JACOBS

THE NEW FRAGRANCE FOR MEN

BANANAMARCJACOBS.COM

Photography

Gaining camera skills and learning about the technical aspects of photography, such as lighting, can be very advantageous if you want to be a fashion stylist. Taking a course that offers both styling and photography is helpful if you are unsure which route to take.

Costume

This is a more specialist route and would be a good choice if you have an interest in working within film, television or in the theatre. Costume courses will include the technical aspects of clothing construction, often incorporating traditional techniques such as corsetry and tailoring.

○ 'Smitten', a Marc Jacobs-inspired perfume campaign.
Styling: Sally Pickering
Photography: Dave Schofield

○ 'Bananaman', another Marc Jacobs-inspired fragrance campaign.
Styling and photography: Ayesha Kiely

Christopher Shannon

Christopher Shannon is a menswear designer. He set up his own label in 2008.

How do you come into contact with stylists in your daily working life?

I started out after college by assisting designers and then stylists, mostly for pop videos and promotional shoots and a few bits of editorial. So that was how I really got to find out how they worked and what goes into the job. Since starting up my own label I come into contact with loads of stylists. Some who just want to borrow samples from the collection for their own shoots or who approach us to make special pieces for music videos. We only really do the ones we want to. On my catwalk show I work with a few stylists who come in for fittings and we talk through all the looks and the models and how we will use the accessories, then also music and lighting. For me it's good to have a few sounding boards that are capable of moving you in a new direction whilst understanding what I am trying to achieve. I will work with someone on pulling together the lookbook shoot and bringing something fresh to that after the clothes have been seen on the catwalk. I like the stylists I work with to also act in a consulting role, bringing me things to look at or extending my research with me.

How do stylists influence you or your work?

I don't look to fashion editorials for inspiration. It depends on the stylist really; it's such a vague title in lots of ways. Some stylists do just the basics and others approach from every angle and include art direction and consulting in their role, which is when the work tends to get more interesting. It's nice when a stylist whose work you like then uses your pieces and presents a fresh interpretation to you; sometimes it can make you see your work in a totally new way.

The fashion stylist

Who, would you say, are the most influential stylists?

For me the first stylist I was aware of, before I really knew what a stylist was, was Judy Blame. Judy had worked with loads of musicians like Neneh Cherry and Bjork, who I was really into as a kid; also he did amazing editorials for *The Face* and *i-D*. He makes a lot of jewellery, which he includes in his shoots and worked a lot with Jean Babtiste Mondino, who I also really like. Judy once told me, 'You should see the person first, then the photograph, then the outfit' when you are looking at an image, which I think is a nice approach. Other stylists I think do interesting work are Jean Paul Goude, who again includes art direction and has produced amazing work with Chanel and also Grace Jones. Also the menswear stylist John Colver (who I work with on my show); his editorials have a really nice sensitivity and he knows the photographers who he works with the best.

In your opinion, what makes a good stylist?

That's tricky because it depends on the situation. As the stylist is often central to bringing a piece of work together I think the best ones are multi-taskers, who are great communicators and have a really fresh personal vision. Being able to control your ego and seeing the bigger picture I think is the best way to make great work.

The images shown here are taken from Christopher Shannon's AW10 lookbook. Art direction by Christopher Shannon with photography by Scott Trindle and styling by John Colver.

A career in fashion styling > Interview: Christopher Shannon > Interview: Deborah Cartwright

Deborah Cartwright

Deborah Cartwright is the managing director of IPR London, a public relations company

How does fashion PR work?

A fashion PR is the person between the designer or brand and the media. They have to think creatively as to how fashion labels will keep momentum within the media. Some fashion designers are already brilliant and press-worthy, so only need to depend on their latest collection to gain press coverage. Some of the bigger and more commercial brands need to keep coming up with new marketing initiatives that will keep them in the press. Sometimes this is the job of the PR, so it helps to have a good sense of marketing and to have a stock of creative ideas that you will know will gain press coverage. We also work with lots of celebrities and musicians who are 'of the moment' and dress them so we can do 'seen wearing' press afterwards. The 'seen wearing' press goes everywhere, which is great for the brand and great for the celebrity, who gets more publicity just because they are wearing a certain pair of jeans!

How does the fashion cycle work?

A fashion year is broken into two seasons: autumn/winter and spring/summer. The launch of a season will happen during the trade shows and then the fashion weeks, so A/W usually kicks off in January at the trade shows and then in February when the fashion weeks start in New York, followed by London, then Milan and Paris. The S/S trade shows happen July and the fashion weeks start in September. It's a constant cycle and never seems to end!

Where do stylists fit into this cycle?

The press (stylists and fashion writers) first see the collections at the fashion or trade shows and then more personal presentations happen a bit later at press days. This is where we set up a showroom with all of the brands and collections and invite the press to come and see the collections up close; it's a good opportunity to meet with the press. Most glossy magazines, such as *Vogue* and *GQ*, work up to four months in advance, so for autumn/winter collections we hold the press day in April. The press come and see the collection and earmark the pieces they want for planned shoots. So something that you see in the September issue of a magazine (which is always the main kick-off issue for autumn/winter collections) may have been shot back in May or June.

We also work throughout the season with press and they come and visit the showroom to choose pieces for their fashion story shoots or still-life shopping pages. Short-lead titles, such as the newspapers and weekly magazines, shoot a bit later in the season and have a quicker turnaround.

Press either come to the showroom and choose a product or they refer to the collection lookbook and choose samples from there. Sometimes you have to prioritize samples for more prestigious publications; for example if a smaller magazine orders a sample and *Vogue* want the same piece at the same time, you obviously have to give it to *Vogue*.

We also meet with the press to plan what we are going to do each season and propose interview ideas and special projects. If a brand advertises with a particular title then you know they have to shoot a certain amount of pieces to gain a good return on investment; so, if a brand advertises eight pages throughout the season with *Glamour*, then *Glamour* has to support the brand with a good amount of what they call 'clippings' of editorial.

Interview: Christopher Shannon > Interview: Deborah Cartwright

WARM LEATHERETTE

Chloé

BARE+BRAZEN

KNOTTED
AND TIED

COMING
UNDONE

Chloé

POWERFUL SENSUALITY

PRADA

MODERN

PRETTY GARCONNE

THE 'BAD' GOOD GIRL

CHIFFON+SILK AGAINST METAL+LEATHER

CORAL ACCENTS

CLASSIC

◐ **Visual research including fashion advertising, photography and filmic references, by Ellie Noble.**

Fashion research, with its close links to visual culture, encompasses many subjects; students should engage with a diverse range of research across a variety of topics. There are two kinds of research: primary and secondary. Primary material is original and doesn't already exist; using your own photography, drawings or conducting interviews first-hand all fall into this category. Secondary research is material that already exists, having been created by someone else; this includes printed and digital research obtained from books, the Internet, magazines, newspapers, journals, reports and other printed material, such as photography, postcards, posters and so on. Undertaking both types of research will give you a broad picture of your subject and related areas, which will drive your work in innovative directions.

○ A collection of art references by Clare Buckley.
Photography: Dave Schofield

'Increasingly, the stylists are becoming the fashion designers' eyes and ears on the world; the secret weapon who pounds the streets in search of interesting reference material, be it the collar on a vintage dress or an obscure artist's monograph.'
Tamsin Blanchard

Essential research

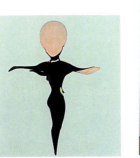

REALLY LOVE THIS IMAGE - SIMPLE & ELEGANT.

couture

DETAILED FULL BODIED TAILORED

Christian Dior, early years...

I CHOP TO LOOK AT THESE PARTICULAR DESIGNS BECAUSE THEY ARE FULL OF MOVEMENT AND COLOUR AND IMMEDIATELY I VISUALISE DETAIL AND THE PASSION ARE SO BEAUTIFUL AND FULL OF DETAIL AND PERFECTION THAT YOU ALWAYS FEEL WOMEN'S WANT TO TOUCH THEM.

ELEGANT, COLOURFUL, FULL SILLOUETTE, SHAPEFUL

CHRISTIAN DIOR - 1951

THESE IMAGES ARE TAKEN FROM A SERIES I BROUGHT IN ACED FROM THE V&M A THESE IMAGES ARE FULL OF COLOUR AND EXTRAVAGANT DETAIL

WARM ELEGANT COLOUR PALLET

BEAUTIFUL DESIGN WHICH FOCUSES ON FLORALS AND WARM FEMININE COLOURS

Dior

Harrods

Christian Dior...

THE MOST INFLUENTIAL DESIGNER OF THE 1940s AND 1950s, DIOR (1905-1957) DOMINATED FASHION AFTER WORLD WAR II WITH THE HOURGLASS SILHOUETTE OF HIS VOLUPTUOUS 'NEW LOOK'.

THE FIRST DIOR COUTURE SHOW WAS SCHEDULED FOR 12 FEBRUARY 1947. DIOR CREATED ELABORATE CLOTHING THAT SHOCKED ALL HIS VIEWERS. THE CLOTHES WHERE THEN NAMED FLOWER WOMEN BECAUSE OF THE UNUSUAL SHAPES AND FABRICS USED.

CHRISTIAN DIOR

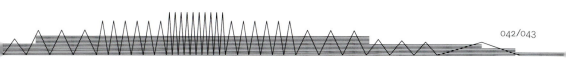
Becoming fashion aware

Fashion has a long and detailed history and it is expected of someone working in the industry, particularly in the fields of design and styling, to be aware at least of the major designers who have innovated and shaped what we wear. Stylists who are concerned with creating work that is innovative and original must know what has been produced previously. Also consider where fashion originated and how economic and social changes have affected the design and manufacture of fashion, such as the austere look of World War II, followed in 1947 by the extravagance of Christian Dior's New Look.

Becoming fashion aware demands that you research all aspects of the industry, from couture to the high street. Examine fashion advertising, visual merchandising, fashion trend pages, street style, fashion articles and interviews, trade reports and trend journals to give you a rounded view of the subject.

⭘ **Research sketchbook pages exploring the work of Christian Dior, by Holly Longhurst.**

Simon Foxton

With a background in fashion design, Simon Foxton is a menswear stylist known for his humorous, street-influenced style of sportswear and tailoring. Fashion director for *Fantastic Man* and consultant fashion director for *i-D* he also contributes fashion stories to *Arena Homme Plus*, *Vogue Homme* and *POP* magazine. Foxton collaborated with Nick Knight on the ground-breaking Levi's campaign, which featured real 'octogenarian ranchers' as models. His styling work was the focus of an exhibition at the Photographers' Gallery in 2009 entitled, 'When you're a boy'.

Fashion editorial for *10 Men*; photography by Will Davidson; styling by Simon Foxton.

Fashion awareness > Fashion communication and culture

Style icons

There are many enduring images of stylish people who have epitomized a designer's vision or reflected the mood or feeling of a particular period: think of First Lady Jackie Kennedy in the famous pill box hat by Oleg Cassini or Bianca Jagger marrying Mick in a Yves Saint Laurent white suit and veiled floppy hat. These style icons continue to be referenced by designers and stylists today. Examine what it means to have personal style and why iconic dress styles from the 1930s or 1960s are still popular today. See the box for a significant list of style icons, past and present, from the worlds of fashion, art, music and acting, to investigate as part of your fashion styling research.

Significant icons

Blondie, Grace Jones, Isabella Blow (stylist), Coco Chanel, Josephine Baker, Jane Birkin, Jackie Kennedy, Chloë Sevigny, Kate Moss, Bianca Jagger, Lauren Hutton, Camille Bidault-Waddington (stylist), Diana Vreeland (fashion editor), Marie Helvin, Paloma Picasso, Bjork, Wallace Simpson, Carine Roitfeld (fashion editor), Anita Pallenberg, Princess Diana, Charlotte Rampling, Marlene Dietrich, Neneh Cherry, Catherine Deneuve, Marianne Faithful, Madonna, Annie Lennox, Jean Shrimpton, Julie Christie, Nancy Cunard, Diane Keaton, Françoise Hardy, Audrey Hepburn, Stevie Nicks, Diana Ross, Farrah Fawcett, Romy Schneider, Marilyn Monroe, Grace Kelly, Jerry Hall, Katharine Hepburn, Edie Sedgwick, Joan Crawford, Brigitte Bardot, Anna Piaggi, Cher, Vivienne Westwood, Maria Callas, Sophia Loren, Joan Collins.

Cary Grant, David Bowie, Alain Delon, David Beckham, Humphrey Bogart, Quentin Crisp, Kanye West, Rudolph Valentino, James Dean, Steve McQueen, Marvin Gaye, Serge Gainsbourg, James Bond, Freddie Mercury, Bob Marley, Jim Morrison, Elvis Presley, Andy Warhol, Ian Brown, Adrien Brody, Prince Charles, Bryan Ferry, The Beatles, Samuel L Jackson, Michael Jackson, Tom Ford, Johnny Depp, Pharrell Williams, Lou Reed, Boy George, Karl Lagerfeld, Paul Weller, Sid Vicious, Jimmy Hendrix, Bob Dylan, Malcolm McLaren.

Street style

Using street style imagery as a research tool illustrates how dress differs around the world. Street style images can be found on dedicated websites, blogs and in magazines. As styling is about the assembly of clothing and accessories, these images illustrate how individual people interpret fashion by constructing and personalizing their dress. You can also take your own street photographs of people whose style you find interesting, which can be a useful source of primary research.

◆ Selection of street style shots from Stylesight.com.
◆ 3D collage of style icon Jerry Hall.
Photography: Dave Schofield
Styling: Jessica Day

Fashion awareness > Fashion communication and culture

Fashion vocabulary

Fashion details are identified through use of colour and silhouette, fabrics and patterns. It is important that stylists are able to identify and describe the many different styles of clothes and accessories as well as the different parts of a garment. Such identifying terms include: type of fabric (cashmere, jersey, chiffon); print (devoré, digital, silk screen); sleeve (bishop, bell, raglan); collar (Peter Pan, button-down, spread); trouser (drainpipe, palazzo, culottes); accessory (turban, deerstalker or boater hat); or silhouette (empire line, trapeze, baby-doll). The correct use of these terms is vital in articulating what items you might require for a photoshoot or if you want to write about fashion.

A good knowledge of colour is equally important. The fashion cycle moves quickly; electric blue changes to royal blue, which moves on to cobalt, so using the right language in relation to colour is important for both stylists and fashion writers. Fashion knowledge will be accumulated through a mixture of research and experience but it will be assumed that as a stylist you possess a fundamental fashion vocabulary.

○ **Fashion editorial for *Russh* magazine.**
Photography: Will Davidson
Styling: Stevie Dance

○ **Stills from a fashion film, *La Vitesse et la Pierre.***
Marcus Palmqvist, Frode Fjerdingstad and Igor Zimmerman

○ **'Dancers', a personal project by Will Davidson.**
Photography: Will Davidson

Handwritten annotations:

snot@ great angle

mystery/un-known/
what's left

collar-layed
are at this different
way

wedding
placed at
foor with
bandages

I want to cover the models face
to make the idea of the unknown
and the unknown nurse much stronger.
I think the image and the concept
would be much more
stronger with the
models face nor
known or seen.

Maison Martin Margiela

The effect of the
lighting hitting the
naked tights on the
face is amazing. It's a whole new take on
headgear – literally.

Context

Your work is about communicating a message through images; to do this effectively you will need a good knowledge of how it will be understood by others in different contexts. A broad understanding of research techniques is essential, such as using the library, making enquiries to experts in any field and searching the Internet for relevant material.

Inspiration

You will stimulate your intellect and creativity by examining a variety of images and literature outside of your personal interests; material that you would not otherwise consume. It is important to keep exposing yourself to new and challenging material throughout your career, to ensure your work is both inspired and inspiring!

○ **Fashion editorial exploring ideas relating to uniform and identity.**
Styling: Ashleigh Chapman
Photography: Charys Ellmer

○ **Sketchbook showing designer research and customization of a nurse's uniform, by Ashleigh Chapman.**

Fashion referencing is a term to describe all of the research elements a stylist brings together to inspire a styling project. Fashion by its very nature means something is in fashion one season and out the next; as such, following trends is always associated with a stylist's work, particularly in editorial. It is understandable, therefore, that students will reference designer collections and fashion magazines in their creation of styling projects. However, it is incorrect to assume that all stylists slavishly follow the trends from season to season. Stylists subconsciously soak up ideas wherever they are and can be inspired by the most obvious or incongruent things. Inspiration can come from visual sources, such as architecture, art or film; it can come from stories or philosophy, such as theories of beauty and aesthetics. References to an individual's upbringing and personal memories are often expressed through a stylist's work: finding connections, themes and developing styling ideas from a somewhat disparate collection of references is a creative and rewarding process.

Fashion references can be collated in several ways. Creating moodboards and sketchbooks are a common but useful way to archive your work and communicate your thoughts. Research can also be compiled digitally on a computer or arranged beautifully on a wall in your workspace.

○ Still-life shoot based on memories by Kate Gearney.
○ Fashion references collected and analyzed to inform styling ideas, by Ellie Noble.

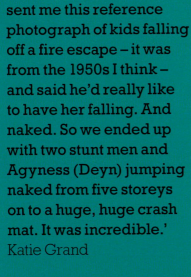

'And then a week later he sent me this reference photograph of kids falling off a fire escape – it was from the 1950s I think – and said he'd really like to have her falling. And naked. So we ended up with two stunt men and Agyness (Deyn) jumping naked from five storeys on to a huge, huge crash mat. It was incredible.'
Katie Grand

Photography

Just as fashion awareness is a prerequisite for stylists, a basic knowledge of photographers and their work is also important. Photography as a creative medium is widely available and inspiration can stem from the composition, colour, mood or narrative in a photograph. Similarly, you can take inspiration from photography that isn't fashion specific. Photography research is easy: there will be plenty of photography books in your local or college library and there are millions of images on the Internet, which are free to view through search engines or image-sharing websites; look out for photography exhibitions in museums and galleries as well. It is good to study the important fashion photographers and be able to recognize their style of work; it is helpful when looking for references. Here is a list of well-known photographers whose work encompasses the photographic fields of fashion editorial and advertising, portraiture, documentary and art.

Influential photographers

Nick Knight, Bruce Weber, Irving Penn, Cedric Buchet, Mario Sorrenti, Mario Testino, Juergen Teller, Wolfgang Tilmans, Peter Lindbergh, Steven Meisel, Man Ray, Herb Ritts, Diane Arbus, Bela Borsodi, Deborah Turberville, Cecil Beaton, Ian Rankin, Tim Walker, Magnus Unnar, Guy Bourdin, David Lachapelle, Richard Avedon, David Sims, Alisdair McLellan, Annie Leibovitz, Corinne Day, Ellen Von Unworth, Patrick Demarchelier, Steven Klein, Mario Sorrenti, Helmut Newton, Inez Van Lamsweerde, Vinoodh Matadin, Craig McDean, Terry Richardson, Mert Alas, Marcus Piggot.

Melanie Ward

In 1989 Melanie Ward collaborated with photographer Corinne Day on the famous gritty shoot featuring a 15-year-old Kate Moss, which changed the direction of fashion (imagery and models were considerably glossier at that time). She subsequently styled the young model for a major Calvin Klein campaign. She took the role of Creative Director at Helmut Lang for 13 years and is now Senior Fashion Editor at *Harpers Bazaar* in New York. In 2009 she launched her own womenswear capsule collection Blouson Noir.

○ **Fashion editorial inspired by the photographic style of Juergen Teller.**
Styling: Daisy Auberson

'I always wanted
people to look as if
they were wearing
their own clothes.'
Melanie Ward

Art

Before photography existed dress styles were documented via artistic impressions, such as drawings and paintings. The composition, subject matter, colour and texture found in paintings, drawings, prints and sculpture are all sources of inspiration for styling. Would-be stylists should know about the significant movements in art and design that have influenced fashion, architecture and furniture design, such as art deco, art nouveau, minimalism and modernism. Surrealism, in particular, heavily influenced fashion design and photography; this can be seen in the collaborative work of artist Salvador Dalí and designer Elsa Schiaparelli or the photography of Man Ray. It is still a strong influence in fashion – think about the exaggerated silhouette in the collections of Victor & Rolf or Shona Heath's set designs in Tim Walker's photographs.

Consider, too, contemporary art practices, such as digital art, performance art and installations; visit museums and galleries to appreciate art firsthand.

◐ **Editorial in which the styling and props were informed by surrealist art.**
Photography: Adam Beazley
Styling: Andrea Billing

◐ **Surreal collage by Jacqueline McAssey.**

Film

The depiction of fashion and style in films is of great value to stylists and continues to provide a great source of inspiration to photographers. Depending on your discipline films may appeal to you on different levels. Films are personal choices and we all have varied tastes: someone may have a passion for American B-movies while someone else may be enthralled by epic costume dramas. Film influences needn't be taken literally, such as copying the costume worn by a character; other cinematic references may be used, such as location or lighting; throughout the film or in a single scene.

The iconic films listed here are suggested viewing. In some instances they define an era, such as *The Great Gatsby*, which portrays dress in the 1920s; others document the styles of a social group, such as mod culture in *Quadrophenia*. Some films have particular fashion connections, such as *Blow Up* (1966), which features an erotic shoot scene with 1960s model Verushka, and *Funny Face* (1957) for which photographer Richard Avedon was a creative consultant. The costumes in *The Fifth Element* (1997) were designed by Jean Paul Gaultier. Fashion designer Tom Ford wrote the screenplay for and directed the film *A Single Man* (2009).

Iconic films

Youth Culture: *The Wild One* (1953); *Rebel Without a Cause* (1955); *Quadrophenia* (1979); *The Breakfast Club* (1985); *This is England* (2006); *Kidulthood* (2006).

Action/crime: *Bonnie & Clyde* (1967); *Mad Max* (1979); *Scarface* (1983); *Top Gun* (1986).

Suspense: *Rear Window* (1954); *The Birds* (1963); *The Thomas Crown Affair* (1968).

Erotic: *Gilda* (1946); *And God Created Woman* (1956); *Belle de Jour* (1967); *American Gigolo* (1980); *Betty Blue* (1986).

Sci-fi: *Metropolis* (1927); *Barbarella* (1968); *Blade Runner* (1982); *The Matrix* (1999).

Romantic: *Roman Holiday* (1953); *Love Story* (1970); *The Way We Were* (1973); *Pretty in Pink* (1986); *Mannequin* (1987); *Pretty Woman* (1990).

Musical/dance: *The Red Shoes* (1948); *An American in Paris* (1951); *My Fair Lady* (1964); *Grease* (1978); *Romeo & Juliet* (1996); *Moulin Rouge* (2001).

Period: *Gone with the Wind* (1939); *Dr Zhivago* (1965); *The Great Gatsby* (1974); *Out of Africa* (1985); *Marie Antoinette* (2006)

Humour/satire: *Blonde Bombshell* (1933); *It Happened One Night* (1934); *The Philadelphia Story* (1940); *Some Like It Hot* (1959); *Breakfast at Tiffany's* (1961); *The Stepford Wives* (1975); *Shampoo* (1975).

◐ ◖ **Film stills from iconic films** *Roman Holiday* (left) and *Blow Up* (above).

Contextual studies > **Fashion referencing**

○ **'Nu Clean' fashion editorial for** ***Oyster*** **magazine.**
Photography: Milos Mali
Styling: Paul Bui

The perceived glamour of working as a stylist is responsible for the surge in styling-related television programmes, magazine articles and college courses. Thanks to its popularity, editorial styling is a highly competitive field. However, with burgeoning online magazines and blogs, there are now many more opportunities to gain editorial experience, along with the prospect of 'self publishing' (this is explored in more detail in Chapter 6).

'I see editorial photography as being about crafting these little separate worlds. It's like creating a little scenario. I'm not sure that's the right word but it's like writing a book and describing an environment. Creating a separate space, a separate reality, is the side of it that I find most interesting.'
Simon Foxton

⬦ **Fashion editorial for** *V Magazine.*
Photography: Will Davidson
Styling: Jay Massacret

Fashion stories

Fashion editorial tells a story through images, often illustrating a theme, mood or concept. Editorial stylists interpret the season's trends, such as the key silhouettes, colours, prints and fabrics through these stories. The fashion editor and their team are responsible for the tone of the fashion editorial and how it will appeal to the readership; the same fashion trend, such as pastel-coloured summer dresses, will be styled and photographed in very different ways according to each publication. The editorial is also determined by the season, such as coats in winter or swimwear in summer.

Alternative publications may offer a more conceptual view of clothing by showing trends that emerge from the street or from art; perhaps a shoot is inspired by an object, the model or the location. Some magazines explore a different theme in each issue, which informs the fashion editorial – or vice versa.

Although more visually stimulating than, for example, a mail order catalogue, fashion editorial is still above all else a selling tool. Editorial trend pages feature outfits that have been put together to inform the reader how to wear trends; often they will show how the look has trickled down from the catwalk to the high street, offering the reader a more affordable version of the trend.

◐ Fashion editorial from the *Guardian: Weekend* magazine.
Photography: Ezra Patchett
Styling: Clare Buckley

○ Womenswear editorial featuring a seasonal animal print trend.
Photography: Jonas Bresnan

◑ ◐ **Womenswear editorial
referencing the work of Yves
Saint Laurent and the
photographic style of
Richard Avedon.**
Styling: Kirsty Geddes

The commercial stylist

The commercial stylist will work with an array of clients on many diverse projects. The client is the linchpin of the commercial project and, as such, the stylist has to be client-focused. The commercial team is often larger than an editorial team. Working alongside the stylist will be the client, who may be someone in the brand's marketing team, or a designer who represents their own label; there may also be an advertising agency representative. There will be a creative team – director, art director, photographer, hair and make-up artist – as well as the models or actors. There may be even more people involved, depending on the brief. It is important for the stylist to be a team player, in order to work with other ideas and suggestions during the creative process.

Editorial styling offers more creative freedom than commercial styling; however, there can be greater financial rewards from advertising projects. It is common at a high level of the fashion industry for stylists who have learnt their craft on magazines to go on and work on major advertising campaigns for international designers and brands; often working with the same team of photographer and make-up artist. This is why the relationships you form with your peers are especially important. A commercial client may approach a experienced photographer to shoot an advertisement, who will then suggest you as the preferred stylist to work on the job.

○ **Advertising campaign for Lanvin for H&M.**
Photography: David Sims

⬙ ⬗ **Advertising campaign for Ellery's A/W10 collection.**
Photography: Holly Blake
Art direction: Kym Ellery

Fashion advertising

Advertisements communicate a message or tell a story to a target market; all of which will be contained within a 'brief'. The client will discuss the brief with the stylist and the creative team before the shoot, in order to begin thinking about the model, location, clothing and props. Sourcing clothing for commercial projects differs from sourcing for editorial: in fashion advertising the images will promote just one brand, retailer or designer and most likely will have already been selected. It is often the fashion buyers, having planned and bought the ranges for a coming season, who will know what the key styles are and what they expect to sell. They, along with representatives from the brand's marketing team, will select these important pieces for the commercial shoot or film.

The focus of this type of commercial advertisement is the clothing or an accessory and as such the visibility of the product is key. The stylist is employed to ensure the clothes are pressed, fit the model well and look their best throughout the shoot. There are, of course, always exceptions. If, for example, an accessories brand wanted to create a fashion advertisement featuring a shot of a model holding a leather handbag, then the stylist would have to source clothing, footwear and jewellery from elsewhere to complete the look, but always in accordance with the client's vision and brief.

Lookbooks

Lookbooks feature pages of fashion products. The stylist will glance through a lookbook and request specific samples for a photoshoot. Occasionally designers will use catwalk images in their lookbooks, otherwise images will be styled just as in any other type of brochure or catalogue.

◒ Lookbook for designer Martine Rose. Art direction by Patrick Waugh.
Photography: Tung Walsh
Styling: Richard Sloan

◒ Accessories lookbook for Lucie Flynn. Art direction by Patrick Waugh.

Styling a non-fashion advertisement

We are exposed to fashion advertising everywhere, but take another look around you. Consider the clothing worn in adverts for companies such as banks or supermarkets. A stylist will have sourced and selected the clothes and styled every person or actor. Commercial stylists will not necessarily follow fashion trends but will know how to develop the clothing for a given character within a commercial brief (see the box, right).

It can be difficult to borrow clothes, unless a stylist has good contacts with PR agencies, because there are no clothing credits. In most cases there will be a budget to allow the stylist to buy the clothing. If more specialist items are needed then appropriate clothing, props and furniture may be hired for a fee. Jobs that require a specific costume, such as a military uniform or ethnic clothing, not only test the stylist's sourcing ability but also their historical and cultural knowledge of dress.

If a high-profile celebrity wears clothing in an advert, the PR representative can generate press (free publicity) for the brand by promoting the fact that the celebrity is wearing the clothes. This type of promotion is called product placement. It also occurs when celebrities wear clothing for television appearances or red carpet events, which is then picked up in the style press.

A typical commercial brief

A common domestic scene is being photographed for a furniture retailer where a mother and child sit on a sofa together reading a book:

■ 'Mother' is 30 years old with light-brown hair and blue eyes. She is a stay-at-home mum, who likes to do activities with her daughter such as baking cakes, painting and reading. Her home is very clean, bright and welcoming but not ultra-modern. She is fashionable but comfort is more important to her. Her favourite clothing and home brands are Jigsaw, Sainsbury's, Laura Ashley and Cath Kidston.

■ Clothing required: size 12; shoe size 6.

■ Props required: selection of books with bright illustrated covers to suit a 4-year-old.

■ 'Daughter' is 4 years old with blonde hair and blue eyes. Her clothes are pretty but practical.

■ Clothing required: size 4 years; shoe size 3.

The shot will convey the lifestyle of the characters within it; therefore the stylist will choose clothes based on their description, and their environment. The sofa is promoted as part of a believable lifestyle that the viewer can identify with.

Editorial styling > **Commercial styling** > Still-life styling

It is not just clothes that drive fashion businesses to economic success. Traditionally, fashion houses have relied on perfume, handbags, shoes, beauty and lifestyle products to generate revenue. Still-life presentation is used within all areas of the fashion industry and it is an essential component in marketing these products for designers and brands.

Catalogue still-life styling tends to be product-focused and may highlight a garment's colour, specific details such as an interesting button or trim, or the choice of colourways available. For editorial or commercial still-life styling there is usually a more conceptual or surreal approach, where the product fits into a story or helps to communicate an advertising message. Beauty products, cosmetics and accessories sit happily in these concepts because of their size.

From catalogues and brochures to e-tailing and online magazines, brands will always need the expertise and flair of still-life stylists to help them display products to their full advantage.

○ Collage-style still-life editorial.
Photography: Jonas Bresnan
○ Still-life beauty editorial 'Paint it pastel' for *Russh* magazine.
Photography: Milos Mali
Styling: Clare Buckley and Kym Ellery

⊙ **A leather glove is the ingredient in this story that focuses on the ritual of afternoon tea.**
Styling and photography: Robyn Winrow

⊙ **The 'jungle' set for this editorial jewellery shoot is made from jigsaw pieces and hand-crafted paper plants and animals.**
Styling: Roseanne Buckler
Photography: David Schofield

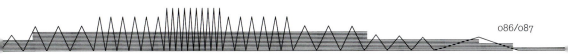

'In still-life photography, everything can be investigated in so many more and different ways. There are endless possibilities and each one of them has the potential to eventually change our perspective.'
Bela Borsodi

Still-life styling

Visual display

Many of the techniques used to display beauty products, clothes and accessories are comparable to those used by visual merchandisers (retail display and window designers). Still-life stylists and visual merchandisers will both consider composition, proportion, scale and the use of colour in a still-life installation.

○ **This still-life set could be used in a 2D image or as a 3D idea for a window display.**
Styling: Kelly Cliff
Photography: James Naylor

○ **The use of a garment's colour and silhouette to form surreal fashion creatures.**
Styling: Kirsty Geddes
Photography: James Naylor

Concepts in still life

Still-life in fashion editorial and advertising is becoming more innovative, artistic and fantastical; it can be difficult to unpick where the styling and photography ends and the computer manipulation begins. On the following pages you will see some creative examples of still-life styling. Some of the clothing and accessories are styled in an unconventional manner, but they are still at the heart of the image.

○ The sock monkey in this playful image is photographed wearing life-size trainers. A photograph of a swing has been converted into an illustration. The final image is achieved by making a digital cut-out of the monkey and placing it on the illustrated background.
Styling and graphics: Roseanne Buckler
Photography: David Schofield

Still-life techniques

The following methods are widely practised in commercial still-life styling. You will find examples in many types of advertisements and in mail-order catalogues and brochures. Still-life stylists have an eye for the smallest detail; they are good at handling and draping fabrics and will have excellent pinning techniques. This method of styling is quite precise and would appeal to those who like to get things just right, although there is an additional pressure of being precise whilst working at a fast pace. Catalogues feature pages and pages of products and you must have the ability to work quickly.

Location

Shooting still-life in a location communicates a lifestyle to suit the product. This lifestyle may be either functional or aspirational.

◐ ◑ Still-life accessory shoot set in an industrial location, which reflects the style of the products.
Styling: Terri Dent
Photography: Mark Prescott

Hanging

A popular method in still-life styling is to hang the garment, either in a studio or on location. This works well when the garment already has a strong silhouette when flat, as illustrated here. Otherwise it will look lifeless, which is commonly described in fashion design and retail as lack of 'hanger appeal'.

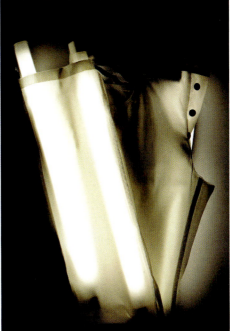

⭘ Menswear still-life using lighting to show the garment's silhouette.
Styling: Danielle Bone
Photography: David Schofield

⭘ Suspending a garment in mid-air using invisible thread.
Styling: Jacqueline McAssey
Photography: David Schofield

Commercial styling > **Still-life styling** > Personal styling

Stack

A stack is used to show a customer the same garment in a variety of colourways. They can be made to look ultra neat or have a purposely crumpled look. The crumpled texture is achieved by arranging tissue paper inside the garment, which allows the stylist to manoeuvre the folds and dents, and keeps them in place for the duration of the shoot. Wadding is also placed between the garments to give the stack more height and avoid sinking, particularly in the centre.

Components

In this layout, the garments and accessories have been styled and photographed separately, presenting the customer with a collection of coordinating garments and accessories. The T-shirts and jacket have been styled using tissue paper to create more body. The scarf has been tied into a shape as if it is being worn. The shoes have been styled and photographed with two different views: one shoe, laid on its side, illustrates colour and branding and the other, shot from above, shows the lace detail.

◐ Although these cardigans appear to be casually stacked, each ridge and dip has been styled to perfection, which requires a gentle touch.
Photography: Alex Hurst
Styling: Carol Woollam

◐ Once these components have been photographed the images are digitally arranged on one page, drawing on colour and branding to give the layout a more graphic look.
Photography: Alex Hurst
Styling: Carol Woollam

◐ This outfit has been arranged on a polystyrene board, which allows the stylist to pin the garments in certain areas to maintain the outfit shape during the shoot.
Photography: Alex Hurst
Styling: Carol Woollam

Outfits

Individual garments can be styled together with shoes, handbags, jewellery or props to make a complete outfit, which is popular with mail-order companies as it helps the less confident customer with their buying decisions. Sometimes the flat outfit may be photographed to the same scale and height as a body to reinforce the 'real person' silhouette. Again, tissue paper is arranged inside the outfit to give the flat garments more shape.

Mannequins

Another way of displaying a garment, such as a shirt, in a more lifelike pose is to use a mannequin. Tissue paper is used to pad and shape the garment and give it a 3D silhouette; arm fullness is created by rolling up tissue paper and forming them under the shirt sleeves. The mannequin can then be digitally cut out of the shot, leaving a more three-dimensional silhouette behind.

Personal styling encompasses image and colour consultancy, one-to-one styling and shopping guidance for private clients or styling advice for the public. This area has seen rapid growth and publicity in recent years, with the rise of the individual 'celebrity' stylist, and the influence that celebrities themselves have on the fashion buying public. Mirroring this trend, it is now common for retailers at all market levels to offer a personal stylist for customers of all ages, shapes and sizes.

Working with private clients relies on the stylist being able to communicate effectively. Having excellent interpersonal skills is the key to a successful styling career and for personal stylists this is critical. Giving style advice to the general public can involve a lot of confidence building as the reasons for a client requiring the services of (and paying for) a personal stylist may be connected to a significant change in their lifestyle, or to more serious issues relating to low self esteem or poor body image. This requires knowledge of the subject and being able to deliver and articulate information in a confident yet empathetic manner. A personal stylist should boost confidence and inspire the client to have a more positive relationship with clothing.

Working with celebrity clients, such as actresses and musicians, may boast a higher level of excitement and glamour but it is wise to consider that they are still individual people with their own insecurities and issues. The major difference is that they will be exposed to greater scrutiny, and criticism, than the average client.

'A stylist needs to know a client's dreams and aspirations, her insecurities and attributes, and how to process all that information to bring out the best and most beautiful in her.'
Rachel Zoe

◐ **Womenswear editorial.**
Photography: Jonas Bresnan

Personal styling for individual clients

The services of a personal stylist are, for many people, an important stage in building self esteem. A successful personal styling appointment should leave the client with firm guidelines on how to manage their own wardrobe by deciding on what styles suit them and what they should look for when shopping alone in the future. For this role the stylist has an assessment with the client to discuss their needs and, more importantly, how the stylist can help them. During the initial meeting with the client, the stylist will consider the following points.

Lifestyle

Clothing has to fit into a client's lifestyle; they may need help with choosing clothing specifically for work, a special occasion, a holiday wardrobe or a complete capsule wardrobe that will work for a whole season. The stylist has to be practical and work with the client by suggesting viable solutions.

Budget

It is important to be able to offer advice based on the client's budget, which requires good research skills and thorough knowledge of the stores and their product offer. It is just as important to research clothing, underwear and accessories at the budget end of the market in addition to the high-end designer collections – and everything in between!

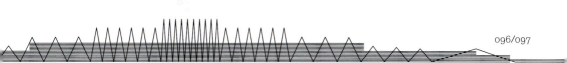

Body shape and age

The stylist establishes the client's height, build, body type and face shape to help the client choose the most flattering clothing and accessories. A client's needs will also vary depending on their age. A stylist can assist with a client's perception of themselves as they age and offer advice on age-appropriate clothing. The stylist can also identify the best colours to wear by examining the client's skin tone and hair colouring; something that changes as a person ages.

Wardrobe weeding

A personal stylist will often carry out a 'wardrobe weeding', which involves sorting through the client's wardrobe, removing any clothes that don't fit, are in a poor condition or are completely out of date. By eliminating these pieces the client will have a smaller selection of suitable clothes and the stylist can then suggest any new purchases to complete the 'new look' wardrobe.

**⟳ ⟲ Womenswear editorial for
Pavement magazine.**
Photography: Adrian Meško

Celebrity styling

There is no doubt that in recent years this form of styling has had enormous publicity. In some instances the celebrity stylists have become celebrities themselves. At a global level these stylists will be very experienced and will have built excellent contacts with both fashion designers and fashion PRs. To be successful in this field requires confidence in your own ability, excellent negotiating skills and the ability to build good relationships with the clients. This is not a 9-to-5 job; many stylists will be called on to provide clothing ideas and solutions to problems at short notice and at any time of the day or night.

There are many reasons for a celebrity client needing the services of a stylist. Practically speaking, if an actress or singer has a busy lifestyle the last thing they are able to do is shop. It is far easier to employ someone who, with an understanding of their taste and style, can research and select the most appropriate styles for them. Celebrity styling is commonly referred to in relation to red carpet events and awards shows. Stylists will, depending on the level of the event, negotiate for months with designer and PRs in order to get their client in the right outfit. Of course, the designer or PR will be selective about who wears their clothing so although it may sound relatively easy, it often isn't.

Stylists often have a signature style, something that makes their work stand out. This, along with their body of work and contacts, may bring them to the attention of a celebrity client. A stylist may be brought in to update or restyle the client, to move them in a new direction. It is often the case that a stylist who builds a rapport with the client, who understands them and their style, is more likely to be rehired.

Celebrity styling may seem out of reach to most stylists starting out, but making contact with and offering your services to unsigned musicians, singers and young actors will provide great opportunities for testing your styling ideas, creativity in sourcing and all-important networking skills.

↻ **Paloma Faith in a photoshoot for the *Guardian: Weekend* magazine.**
Photography: Ezra Patchett
Styling: Clare Buckley

Still-life styling > **Personal styling** > Interview: Siobhan Lyons

Styling musicians

Stylists are often hired to prepare a musician or singer for a special event, such as a tour, or to provide ideas for an album cover or music video. To some extent bands and musicians will look for something that fits with them and their music. As in commercial styling, sourcing clothes can be easy or difficult depending on the client. Some designers are more than happy to lend their clothes to be worn in a video but it depends if the designer or brand is a good fit with the client and whether or not they will receive publicity from the relationship.

'I think that the role of the stylist is to be in the middle of it and get everyone together to make it happen!'
Nicola Forminchetti

○ Behind the scenes on a Lady Gaga shoot.
○ Fashion editorial influenced by the music scene.
Photography: Milos Mali

Nicola Forminchetti

Of Italian and Japanese descent Forminchetti credits his eclectic and prolific fashion work to this global upbringing. He is fashion director of *Vogue Homme Japan* and contributing fashion editor at *Dazed & Confused*, *Another Magazine*, *Another Man*, *V Magazine* and *V Man*. He also consults with brands Uniqlo and Y3, and designers Giorgio Armani and Prada.

Perhaps one of his most influential roles is that of stylist to musician Lady Gaga. He is responsible for her radical look, styling her magazine shoots and music videos.

Siobhan Lyons

Siobhan Lyons began her career as assistant stylist to Jacob K

Starting out

I did an art foundation course followed by a fashion degree at Leeds College of Art and Design. I moved to London six months after finishing my degree; on my own, with no job, nowhere to live and I knew one person. I wanted to do styling and be more involved in fashion and London was the only place to be.

I started working in Gareth Pugh's studio on his catwalk collection for A/W08. After that, I spent days e-mailing magazines looking for internships. Eventually I got a response and began interning at *Another Magazine*.

Interning is about gaining people's trust and showing that you are reliable, responsible and willing to learn. Yes, I made tea, and yes, I did a lot of what seemed like 'thankless' tasks, but inevitably they all lead to something more worthwhile. I'm glad I stuck it out or else I don't think I would have had all the valuable experience I have now.

Assisting Jacob K

I met Jacob K and became his first assistant for the next two and a half years. You become their second 'brain'; begin to think like them and have to learn to be ten steps ahead.

As an assistant you spend a lot of time e-mailing and on the phone chasing things up with PRs. It's very difficult as Jacob is not the only stylist shooting. There are hundreds of stylists all shooting at the same time and who all want the same things! It is extremely stressful and things don't always go to plan.

You have to give up a lot; it's hard to make plans around work as the schedule will change all the time. Sometimes you are on the road for weeks at a time, shooting back to back. Travelling is one of the best things about assisting; I have been so fortunate to go to amazing places all over the world and assist on jobs and meet people I'd never even have dreamed of. I never knew that I'd begin by tearing up tear sheets and end up doing what I did. I have been very lucky indeed.

Portrait of Siobhan Lyons photographed by Tim Walker.

Personal styling > Interview: Siobhan Lyons > Interview: Emma Jade Parker

Siobhan Lyons

Working on a Tim Walker shoot

This shoot was a Tim Burton retrospective, so we were basically going to recreate some of the iconic characters in his films. I had to research fetishwear, find latex cat masks, gloves, stockings. Jacob had selected all the looks he wanted from various designers and catwalk shows; it was then my responsibility to request all these things from various PRs and keep track on their availability.

On this shoot we had 12 trunks arrive from the US from *Harper's Bazaar*. We also had eight suitcases of our own. It is the most we have ever had on a shoot. We shot in the rose fields of Colchester, UK, so we had to set up everything in the barn; not an ideal situation as it was quite dark and dirty, but we managed.

There was a 100 ft skeleton that had been made especially for the shoot, suspended from a crane. I ended up wearing a Martin Margiela all-in-one bodysuit, some crippling knee-high Alexander McQueen boots, and was wrapped head to toe in bandages with a huge mask as the character Jack Skeleton from *The Nightmare Before Christmas*.

These images are from the Tim Burton shoot for *Harper's Bazaar*. Photography by Tim Walker; set design by Shona Heath; styling by Jacob K; assistant stylist Siobhan Lyons.

A day in the life of a commercial assistant

Setting up

A typical day would start with a crew call for breakfast any time between 6am and 8am. The shoot could be in a studio or out on a location. If we are shooting in a studio I would have a wardrobe room to set up in. On location I could be on a wardrobe truck, which is essentially a converted van with rails, sink, a washing machine and so on, or inside the unit base, which could be anywhere from a pub to a church or house!

My first job is to unpack and hang the clothing and accessories and fill up the steamer and iron with water. I work closely with the hair and make-up artist to create a look for the actor, model or presenter. The production usually set a timed schedule for the artist to get ready in but if we feel the artist should have make-up first or get into their wardrobe first then we make the decision.

Sometimes the artist may be wearing something delicate that I wouldn't want creasing by sitting in make-up for an hour and production may not know this when they produce the schedule. A big part of the job is to be practical and always thinking ahead. If we have not had a fitting prior to the shoot day then I will do one first thing in the morning to get approval for the outfit; then, while the artist is in hair and make-up, I will press the clothing and hang it, ready to be put on at the last minute.

There are several people who need to approve the clothing: the director; the advertising agency, who writes the concepts; and the client. This requires good people skills, a positive attitude and the ability to explain your choices and back them up in an intelligent and educated manner. There are many opinions; however, it's good to remember you are the stylist and this is your field of expertise.

Sectors within styling

'A big advantage is having good observational skills and absorbing everyday, commonplace information from style and fashion to music, film and culture.'
Emma Jade Parker

Emma Jade Parker

Working on set

Once the artist is called on set I will go with them and watch the action on the monitor, making sure they look perfect and looking out for any wardrobe malfunctions and continuity issues. Sometimes we can film the artist walking through a door on location on day one and walking out the other side in the studio on day two, so it is essential that the continuity of the clothing matches exactly: the handbag must be in the same hand; the amount of buttons done up must be identical; the scarf must be tied the same way.

The length of day can vary but generally we would work a 10- or 12-hour day on-camera. At the end of the day I pack everything down and organize the clothes that need to be returned to the stores, hire companies or PR companies.

Aspects of the job

I have a returns or 'de-prep' day to take any clothing back. I also organize my receipts and make sure that everything I have spent tallies with the money I have remaining: managing the budget is a big part of my job as is the prep. I would receive a brief, director's treatment, storyboards, moodboards, artists' sizes and budget information so I can do all of the buying. I mainly purchase the clothing if current trends are needed but sometimes I hire, make or borrow clothing too. It is, of course, essential to be fashion and style conscious and follow trends but it is also necessary to have a solid understanding of fashion and costume history and street style from all walks of life.

Interview: Siobhan Lyons > Interview: Emma Jade Parker > Interview: Carol Woollam

Carol Woollam

A day in the life of a still-life stylist

The briefing

As a still-life stylist my clients are mainly mail-order companies. A briefing will have taken place a couple of days or even a week or so prior to the shoot, with the art director, photographer and stylist present. A buyer and/or designer may also be at the briefing if there is a particular detail that needs to be shown or product that needs to be photographed. The briefing will determine how many products will be shot each day; the type of lighting required by the photographer and what props or backgrounds are needed, which will have to be sourced and in the studio ready for the first day of the shoot.

The amount of products to be shot in a day is normally achievable and it can vary from client to client. Some clients have a low-shot rate and low-density pages (fewer products) as the photograph will be used as a selling shot. Other clients will require a quicker turnover; their pages will normally be of a higher density (more products) and will have a model shot as the selling shot.

On the shoot

The budget will have been set by the client and will include photographer, stylist and assistant fees (sometimes a set builder) studio and equipment hire, food and drink and transport.

A typical day on a still-life shoot would start between 8.30 and 9am. When I arrive at the studio, I unpack my styling kit, set up the ironing board and iron and have the steamer filled with water and ready to go. Preparing the products in advance will allow you to foresee any problems that may arise. It also allows you to check that the products are correct, particularly the size and colour. Depending on the type of garment and how it is being presented, I will press or steam and fold it, if required, ready to place on set.

The creative team will sit down and discuss the order of photography. While the photographer is setting up the lights and set, I will arrange the clothes on the garment rail in the order they are to be shot. If there are both single and multi-product shots, it is usually easier to start prepping the single items to get ahead and give you more time to prep on the bigger shots.

When the garment is placed on the set, a quick snap is taken and viewed on screen to check that it is in position; if correct the adjustments can then be made. If the garment requires movement, this can be created by using tissue and wadding. Continuous shots are taken until the lighting and product look correct. The art director will overlook the final shot and point out any fine-tuning that needs to be done. A close-up view on the computer screen can reveal any faults that can be corrected.

Sometimes things may not go according to plan and a shot may not work, so clear and constant communication is imperative at all times between the creative team so you are all working on the same level. If the stylist or photographer can foresee any problems with the shot, it should be brought to each other's attention immediately and resolved quickly to ensure that deadlines are met.

Interview: Emma Jade Parker > Interview: Carol Woollam

⊙ **Fashion editorial for *Russh* magazine shot on location at Bondi Beach, Australia.**
Photography: Milos Mali
Styling: Clare Buckley

In order to embark on a career in fashion styling you will need to build a body of work that you can show to prospective employers or clients. If you are not assisting a professional stylist then producing work by means of a 'test' is the best way to try out your ideas. This method allows you to produce images on a minimal budget by working with photographers, hair and make-up artists and models for free. In addition to developing your portfolio this helps you build confidence and develop a more professional way of working. There are many factors to consider when styling a fashion shoot and they don't always go to plan. However, if you are only testing and trying ideas, it doesn't matter as much; it is beneficial to make mistakes early on and to learn from them. A stylist needs to react and adapt to problems and changes that occur during the image-making process. How you deal with these challenges is a key part of the job.

○ Fashion editorial shot in Paris for *Rodeo* magazine.
Photography: Marcus Palmqvist and Frode Fjerdingstad
Styling: June Nakamoto

○ Behind the scenes of a fashion editorial; the roles of styling, art direction and photography are divided between students.
Photography and styling: Samantha Grayer, Charlotte Jackson and Tara Bamforth

Organizing a test shoot

A test shoot is a trade-off; you are all working together to one common aim which is to get usable images for your portfolios. If you are studying an art and design course you will be surrounded by creative students in disciplines such as photography, fashion, textile design, graphic design and illustration. It is up to you to seek out people and establish a working creative team. This is also the first step toward networking which, admittedly, some people find easier than others. If you don't have the confidence to approach people, then think about advertising yourself and skills, by way of posters or through websites and online groups. Finding like-minded people to work with is imperative and the relationships you make early on in your career can stay with you throughout your professional working life. Ultimately, an ideal team is one in which all members have ideas that merge; one in which everyone works towards the overall art direction.

While you are encouraged to collaborate with other creative people to produce images it is by no means impossible to produce images yourself. You may wish to take your own photographs, which is possible on small-scale shoots. By using a digital camera, your own clothes and by shooting in a friend's house or an outdoor space, you can style and produce shots and begin to analyze your own styling work. You will find, however, that the greater the number of scenes or shots, outfits and models, the more difficult becomes the dual role of stylist and photographer. Primarily, a stylist takes care of the clothing and needs to focus on this throughout the shoot. Take your eye off the ball and problems can be missed, until you see them in the final photograph when they cannot be rectified or corrected digitally. In fact, even at the test stage, the production of your shoot may be large enough for you and your photographer to need assistants.

Communication

The complex organization and planning involved for photoshoots requires excellent communication and negotiating skills. The more people involved, the more lines for communication are needed. Some shoots can take weeks to plan and develop; others progress quickly. If specific props have to be sourced or made, or there are special locations to be found, the stylist must undertake a copious amount of planning. Advances in mobile and web technology and the use of social networking and file-sharing websites, such as Flickr or Facebook, have all made the organization of a shoot faster and more fluid, particularly for students. Camera phones are useful for casting models or photographing inspirational references to use in a shoot.

Stills from a 1960s-inspired shoot.
Styling: Kelly Cliff
Photography: Alexander Lockett

Preparing for a photoshoot

Studio

Shooting in a controlled environment means not having to worry about the lighting or weather, as you would if you were outside. College studios will normally be equipped with lighting, cameras, computers, backdrop paper and props, as well as hair styling equipment, mirrors and clothes rails. Hair and make-up can be done either in or near the studio and models will have somewhere to change clothes in relative comfort. Add some music and it is possible to generate an energetic or relaxing ambience during the shoot proceedings.

Using the studio as a blank space, without props or furniture, places the emphasis on the lighting, clothing, model and poses. If you don't have access to a studio then you may want to choose an interior space that resembles a 'blank canvas'.

O Using the studio as a blank canvas places emphasis on the model and the clothing.
Styling: Stephanie Cherlet
Photography: Sally Ashley-Cound

On location

◐ Shot on location at the Hotel Concorde Opéra in Paris for the *Guardian: Weekend* magazine.
Photography: Ezra Patchett
Styling: Clare Buckley

Shooting on location can add colour and glamour, a sense of decay or a feeling of familiarity. If you are open to using any location then consider your surroundings. Take a fresh look at where you live, work or study. An effective location can be as ordinary as your own garden or kitchen. Always have a camera with you so you can take a photograph when you see an inspirational location; remember to note where it is.

If it's a complete look you want then hotels offer many different types of interior that are fully furnished. If you are looking for a real home to shoot in, then consider approaching an estate agent who may let you use an empty or furnished property or ultra-modern show home.

Another point to remember is how many scenes you want from your shoot. Does the location have enough detail to get the amount of different scenes you want? Open spaces such as parks and woodland offer impressive views and a variety of different settings for one shoot, whereas one small room may be limiting. Shooting outside is also affected by the light so this also has to be considered; the weather is the uncontrollable variant in any outdoor shoot.

The first steps in trying to shoot at a location are simple. Make contact with the relevant person, usually a manager. Explain what you are doing and that the photographs are for your portfolios. Make clear exactly what you need and, more importantly, how long you will need the space for. Locations such as cafes and hotels are working businesses and need to keep running during your shoot; they may suggest a quieter time for you to use the space. The more organized and professional you appear, the more trust and confidence will be placed in you.

A note of caution regarding location work: permission or special permits will most certainly be required when shooting on someone else's property. It may be impossible to shoot in government-owned buildings; places of national importance; or in public places, such as swimming pools or train stations. Permission to shoot in open spaces such as parks and beaches may also be required, especially if they are in protected conservation areas. Always do your research; if you don't, you could risk being removed from the location, which will threaten the shoot and waste the team's time and money.

Similarly, derelict properties, with their decaying interiors, are always attractive to stylists and photographers but you must consider the dangers of shooting in or around such a building.

When considering working at a location it is imperative to have a plan B should the weather make it impossible to shoot or if there is a change of plan. When looking at possible locations look around the area for alternative places to move to. If, for instance, you are planning a shoot in a park, look for a covered area you could move to should it rain.

○ **Fashion editorial for *Russh* magazine shot on location.**
Photography: Milos Mali
Styling: Tamilla Purvis

○ **Fashion editorial capturing a model and real people in an outdoor location.**
Styling: Kelly Cliff and Kirsty Geddes
Photography: Alexander Lockett

We have already established that this area is the remit of the fashion stylist. How and where you source clothing will depend on your continued energy, resourcefulness and networking ability. As well as sourcing items for a shoot a stylist will bring a reserve of clothing and accessories, which may be vintage finds from their own wardrobe or pieces that have been amassed over time on previous shoots. Usually they are classic pieces of jewellery or belts, scarves and sunglasses. Basic clothing, such as a plain white T-shirt or shirt, is also good to have. These extra pieces can often fill in the gaps during a shoot where you need, but don't have, another option; an alternative colour or different shape. In addition, the model's own clothes should also be used as a resource. Ask them to bring general items such as jeans, vests and T-shirts, plus any specific items you can think of. Footwear is always difficult to source and if the model has large or very small feet it is helpful if they bring a range of styles to the shoot.

'These days there are so many ways to find quality at accessible prices, from eBay to second-hand shops.'
Rachel Zoe

Making contacts

Being a stylist is all about making contacts in fashion and working with designers. The best place to start is where you live; expand your contacts book by finding fashion designers, jewellery makers, milliners and shoemakers that are local to you. If you are at college then you are probably surrounded by creative students producing a diverse range of clothing and accessories. Tapping into this great resource means you will have access to original clothing that won't have been used or seen before. Sourcing further afield, young designers can also be discovered at end-of-year college shows and exhibitions or at national events.

Clothing, accessories and footwear brands and designers can also be found at business trade shows, such as Bread & Butter and Prêt à Porter Paris. Fashion week events in London, New York, Paris and Milan don't generally allow students to attend the fashion shows or exhibitions, although this won't necessarily deter the most resourceful student from gaining access.

◔ Clothing and accessories can be sourced from anywhere; how you go about sourcing will depend on your energy and resourcefulness.
Photography: Jacqueline McAssey

Sourcing clothes

Vintage or second-hand clothing

Second-hand shops, car-boot sales, flea markets, vintage fairs and retail websites, such as eBay, are all great places to find period clothing and accessories, and they should be relatively inexpensive. The point of sourcing items in this way is not that you find a rare vintage piece but that you find something that resonates with you, something that fits with the story you are working on and that is above all else, unique. Specialist vintage shops that sell antique jewellery or original pieces by recognized designers are usually expensive, but it may still be possible to find the genuine article, at the right price, from time to time.

Family and friends

In a similar way to sourcing in second-hand shops it's always advisable to explore the wardrobes of your friends and family. Consider how many aunts and grandmothers keep hold of their clothes for sentimental reasons or because they haven't got round to sorting through them. Likewise, their antique jewellery can be a welcome, unique addition to your shoot. However, using other people's clothes and jewellery, which are probably irreplaceable, brings responsibility.

Buying and returning clothes

As a team you may agree on a small budget for clothing and accessories but this can be used up quite quickly. As sourcing can be difficult when starting out, it is common practice to buy clothes from shops and return them. However, there are some stores that will not accept certain items of clothing, such as underwear, swimwear or tights. Similarly, earrings are usually non-returnable in most stores. It is up to you to determine the best method for you and your team and remember that the clothing is the responsibility of the stylist: ensure that the store accepts returns and make a note of the terms and conditions; be extremely organized with the packaging and carrier bags and, most importantly, the receipts. Keep them in a safe place and make a note of which receipt goes with each item.

Customizing

Customization can mean anything from dyeing clothing to pinning, pleating, folding, cutting and slashing a garment to give it a new look. Reworking items in this manner is a creative way of reinventing a garment and it works well when you use inexpensive, basic pieces. The addition of embroidery, beads, gems or simply drawing on a garment can revamp plain clothing; also consider using transfer paper, which allows you to design and apply your own prints. In addition to haberdashery you could try customizing clothes with items found in hardware stores: wiring, tape; even nuts and bolts can all be used on clothing and in photoshoots. If you have a background in fashion design, pattern cutting or construction, you can approach customization in a different way, such as deconstructing clothing – unpicking seams, removing sleeves and collars – to construct a wholly different outfit, thus creating something unique to shoot.

◐ ◑ Putting looks together using clothes sourced from vintage shops and markets.
Styling: Clare Buckley

As the stylist you will be heavily involved in sourcing the props when you are starting out. In the absence of a budget, which would allow you to hire from a prop house, you will have to use your negotiating skills to the full. Being creative is a constant but rewarding challenge. Producing a shoot without a budget will test your creativity but, if you are going to succeed as a stylist, creativity will be your biggest asset.

◐ ◑ **Creative use of everyday props: a wooden spoon and potted plants.**
Photography: Milos Mali
Styling: Clare Buckley

Second-hand props

Second-hand shops, car boot sales and websites are good sources for imaginative and bizarre props that you would otherwise only find in a prop house. As with clothing, second-hand furniture and props may be sourced and customized. For a small donation, some charity shops (thrift stores) may let you use the furniture and then return it after a shoot. Inexpensive furniture can be painted or distressed to suit your needs. However, you will need to arrange transportation of large items to the studio or location. All manner of homewares and furnishings, such as vases, ornaments and cushions, can be sourced second-hand. Paintings, photographs and frames also give a room set a new look. Everyday items such as magazines, books, flowers and plants are easy to source but often you will need a specific prop for a shoot and this is where your research skills will be put to the test. Use the Internet – websites such as eBay – to search for even the most obscure props.

Sourcing clothes > **Props and set design**

Changing a location

Creating a set in a studio could involve painting a wall, laying a floor and moving furniture into the space. Alternatively, as photographs capture a moment in time, it is possible to temporarily change an environment for a shoot and most rooms can be restyled to some degree. By moving or covering furniture and removing pictures from walls you can change the look of the set; wallpaper or backdrop paper can be hung temporarily and fabric can be draped in imaginative ways. When the shoot is over the location can be restored to its original state. Whatever you decide to do, you will probably need the team or an assistant to help you.

Ready-made props

Locating a space containing the perfect props saves a lot of time and is easier than borrowing or hiring expensive props or trying to create a room set inside a studio. Hotels and stylish apartments offer stylists the opportunity of working in modern spaces that are already dressed with high-end products, such as modern lighting, flat-screen televisions or state of the art music systems.

⊘ Creating a location in the
studio using different
materials.
Photography: Alexander Lockett

⊘ Dressing a location with an
eclectic mix of personal items.
Styling and photography: Holly
Ashbrook

⟲ **Fashion editorial mimicking the shoot process.**
Photography: Milos Mali

All fashion shoots will need forward planning to ensure the day runs as smoothly as possible. Who takes the role is up to the team to discuss but production planning can often be split between the photographer and stylist, or another person can be brought on board should the job become too big. Consider the following production issues:

- First, is everyone available? It can be problematic if the creative team or the model are studying and have to squeeze the shoot in alongside studying or work.

- Permission to shoot at a location should be arranged during the production stage. Make sure the team has identification or a letter of authority agreeing that the shoot can take place. Always save email correspondence and take it with you.

- Take note of the size of the location, particularly indoor spaces. Logistically, how will the shoot work if there is a large group of people involved?

- Locate electrical points for equipment such as cameras, lighting and laptops.

- Are there any changing facilities for the model? Are there toilets available?

- Think about transport for the creative team, models, clothes, equipment and any props. If you are driving, is car parking available and is it free of charge? Do permits have to be arranged in advance?

Apples signify peace and salvation, they also symbolise the temptation into sin and the choice between good and bad.

Surrealism

surrealism definition
an avant-garde 20th-century movement in art and literature which sought to release the creative potential of the unconscious mind, for example by the irrational juxtaposition of images

Sophie Gibson

Model:
Amaryllis
Height: 5' 2"
Hair Colour: Red

Photographer:
Amanda Littler
www.amandalittler.co.uk

The colour red is a strong, hot colour which symbolises many conflicting emotions such as love, sin and violence. Red symbolises Cupid but also the Devil. It is recognised as a stimulant provoking excitement & energy but also a sense of protection from fears and anxiety.

Jenni Boyle - 1st year photography

Models & Photographer

Hair & Makeup

We looked at surrealist such as: Maggy Taylor, Philip Treacy Couture, Salvador Dali, Jodis Eirsdottir and Meret Oppenheim because it linked with the dream/fantasy narrative that we wanted to create.

Mary Antoinette was the inspiration for the style hair and makeup, we felt the clothes reflected this era. This took on a darker more exaggerated look when we looked at surrealism.

xhibition guide

ngels of Anarchy
omen Artists and Surrealism
6 September–10 January
anchester Art Gallery

⬥ A series of moodboards by Danielle Bone, Lindsay Walton and Francesca Adams, reflecting the many stages of a photoshoot: inspiration; location; model choices and ideas for hair and make-up.

Equipment

The type of equipment you will need very much depends on where you are working. A well-equipped studio will have apparatus such as rails, irons and steamers so you won't need to source and transport them to the shoot. If you are going to use a studio that you've not worked in before always check what equipment is there; don't assume it will have everything you need. Shooting on location will be quite different. You may have to bring all relevant equipment with you as well as the clothing and accessories, which can take up a lot of space; it all needs to be methodically organized.

A stylist should have a range of indispensable small items that they can easily transport from job to job, usually in a utility box or bag. If you are an art and design student you will own most of these items already.

A basic styling kit

- Scissors in various sizes and for different materials, such as fabric, paper
- Tape measure
- Straight pins, safety pins
- Clamps in various sizes, to temporarily adjust and secure garments that are too big
- Needles and various colour threads
- Masking tape to protect the soles of borrowed shoes
- Double-sided tape to secure or repair hems
- Cleavage/lingerie tape to keep clothing in place on the body
- Invisible nylon thread is good for hanging clothing; it is frequently used in still-life styling and visual merchandising
- Stitch unpicker to unpick hems and seams
- Steam iron
- Ironing board and sleeve board – these should be lightweight and portable
- Lint roller or clothes brush to remove unwanted hairs and fibres from clothing
- Hangers
- Garment bags to protect and organize clothing in transit and during shoot
- Bags or suitcases on wheels to transport clothing, accessories and sundries

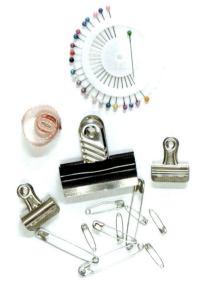

◎ ◎ **A selection of basic styling equipment, a small hand-held steamer and a steam iron.**

You may decide to invest in more expensive equipment as and when you need it. Garment steamers are easy to use and perfect for garments with an intricate construction or delicate details. They are fitted with large water tanks, which means you can steam clothes for much longer than you would if using a small domestic iron. Professional steamers are expensive; less expensive are the compact or hand-held versions, which hold less water. Garment rails on wheels are ideal for hanging and organizing the clothes before and during a photoshoot. Rails vary in size and cost; it is possible to buy domestic-use rails from high street stores, or sturdier professional rails from fashion retail suppliers. Ideally any rails you use should be collapsible or break down easily to fit into a car should you have to take it on location.

Photographic equipment is really the concern of the photographer. Along with cameras and lighting they may want different types of lens, reflectors, ladders and so on. If you are lucky, your photographer will own some or all of the kit needed. If not, equipment can be borrowed from friends or a college store or rented from a camera hire shop. If you are shooting outdoors or in a space that doesn't have electricity then you will also need battery packs to power the equipment. Again, the photographer will establish this.

If all this equipment has to be moved to location then arranging reliable transport is crucial, as is the security of such items. Never leave valuable equipment on show or unattended in cars or in public locations. If it's not possible to keep it all with you, assign an assistant to watch over it during the shoot.

It is imperative to communicate with the team before the shoot in order to consolidate ideas, so if possible, arrange a meeting for all team members. The meeting should be used to recap the ideas and visual references for the overall mood of the shoot, model casting, location choices and poses; there should also be a final discussion regarding clothing, hair and make-up choices. The meeting should leave everyone with a clear outline of the story and the day itself.

It is also useful, particularly for the photographer, to undertake photographic tests in preparation for the final shoot. A friend or assistant, if the model isn't available, can assume the role of the model, standing in the location or studio space as the model would. The photographer will then do a series of test shots, arranging the lights in order to achieve the desired effect and working out a plan for the day. If both the model and the clothes are available then it is possible to do a full mock shoot, where all ideas can be put into practice, knowing changes can still be made. The mock images may then be reviewed by the team and any alterations suggested for clothes, make-up, lighting and location before the final shoot.

◐ **Testing colour and lighting ideas for a photoshoot.**
Styling and photography by Andrea Billing and Kate Geaney

Call sheet

The photoshoot is a complex production and brings together a number of people, clothing, props and equipment; in order to synchronize all these elements a call sheet should be used. A call sheet provides details of the creative team, including assistants; their names and roles on the shoot, along with their contact details. The document will also specify a 'call time', which is when the shoot begins, the location and address, transport details, maybe a map of the location and any catering details.

To aid time management it should also act as a timetable, showing the shoot broken down into practical timeframes; if, for example, 10 shots are required, this equates to five in the morning and five in the afternoon. This keeps the team on track during the event. Special requirements are also recorded on the call sheet, such as, for example, 'Can model please bring black, high-heeled shoes.' The document should then be e-mailed, faxed or handed to each member of the team a day or two in advance of the shoot.

It is a professional mode of working and makes perfect sense when trying to get everyone and everything to the right place at the right time. For instance, if a member of the crew is running late or finds that they are lost on the way to the location they can refer to the address or map on the call sheet or call a member of the team for further directions.

Call sheet for 'American Gigolo' shoot

Shoot date: 25th October 2010

Call time: 9am–7pm studio

Location: UCLAN Media Factory

Contact: Clare Buckley

Photographer: Dave Schofield

Photo assistant: John Butterworth

Stylist: Clare Buckley, tutor; 2nd year fashion promotion with styling students

Stylist assistant: 2nd year fashion promotion with styling students

Models: Amadine, Julie, Coco

Model chaperones: Danielle Bone and Kirsty Geddes

Hairstylist: Martyn Jones

Make-up: Jurgen Gregory

Catering: Clare Buckley and the fashion promotion styling team will supply food and drinks

Day schedule:

8.45am: chaperones pick up models

9am: team arrive at studio

9.15am–10.30am: hair and make-up, shoot set up

10.30am–11am: styling

11am: shoot begins; shot 1, shot 2, shot 3

1pm: lunch for all crew

2pm–5pm: shot 4, shot 5, shot 6

5–6pm: crew clean up and pack studio

5.15pm: chaperones transport models to train station

Diana Vreeland (1903–1989)

Diana Vreeland was a magazine editor and fashion icon. She reinvented the job of fashion editor at *Harper's Bazaar*, where she worked for over 25 years: she chose the clothes and oversaw the photography. She went on to become Editor in Chief at *Vogue* and then consultant to the Costume Institute of the Metropolitan Museum of Art.

'[Diana Vreeland] was and remains the only genius fashion editor.'
Richard Avedon

⊙ **Fashion editorial for the**
***Guardian: Weekend* magazine.**
Photography: Ezra Patchett
Styling: Clare Buckley

Editing the clothes

The process of selecting and editing clothes is probably the most magical part of the fashion stylist's role. Preparation and organization are key; the more time you have with clothes beforehand the more you can experiment with the looks and perfect your ideas. Editing prior to a shoot can also help determine if something won't work or if alternative items have to be found. Unfortunately, however, it is not uncommon for borrowed clothes to arrive the day or night before a shoot or even on the day itself, particularly if they've been sourced from local designers or retailers. Similarly, if you have asked the model to bring clothes to the shoot you might not see them until they arrive on the day. Stylists often work with clothes that they have not seen close up, if at all, and the ability to think on your feet constitutes a major part of the stylist's qualities.

When you take delivery of the clothing, make a detailed list of what has been borrowed and where it is from. Unpack all the clothing and hang it on rails or on a clean floor. Start the editing process by putting ideas of looks together, keeping the shoot story in mind. Then try each outfit on the model or a friend; clothing looks different when worn. Fully accessorize your choices with jewellery, shoes and hosiery. Finally, take a photograph of each option, not only to remind yourself but also to show the team on the day of the shoot.

The more prepared you are, the more creative you can be on the shoot. Looks can change when placed in the environment and what you originally envisaged may not work. Edit clothes that are not right, but do make sure you take alternatives to help your styling on the day. Finally, all clothes should be pressed, placed on hangers and in garment bags, ready to transport to the location.

⊙ **Two looks from a fashion editorial entitled 'Femme'.**
Photography: Anton Zemlanoy
Styling: Marsha Vetolskiy

As a key member of the photoshoot the stylist has to work hard to ensure that it runs as smoothly as possible. A shoot can descend into chaos quite easily as more people arrive and their bags and coats are removed and clothes and equipment are unloaded. Follow studio etiquette at all times; this means abiding by the studio or location rules. Food or drink is not usually allowed in studios. Shoes should not be worn when walking on paper backdrops, so work barefoot or wear socks. Also, be prepared for bad weather in outdoor locations, take waterproofs, blankets and hot drinks in flasks to ensure the model is warm and comfortable.

Hair and make-up usually takes longer than expected so the earlier you can start the better. Where possible find a space to arrange clothes, accessories and shoes, on rails or tables. Try to arrange everything so you can see it all; you can easily forget about what you have sourced. Check the clothes and assess those that need further steaming. Place the clothes in order and arrange the accessories that go with each outfit. If you have time, check the fit of the clothes on the model, particularly if there has been no previous opportunity for a fitting; otherwise you can do this quickly in between shots.

○ Fashion editorial showing model in a mock photoshoot.
Photography: Marcus Palmqvist and Frode Fjerdingstad
Styling: June Nakamoto

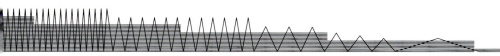

Working with the photographer and model

Discuss with the team the look you are shooting first and dress the model. The model will stand in the space and the photographer will start shooting to determine if the lighting and camera settings are correct. When the photographer is ready to start, you can make final adjustments to the clothes. By clamping or pinning the clothes at the back you can alter the silhouette of the garment, drawing it in at the waist or hips. Be sure to tell the model what your role is; what it entails and that it is you, as the stylist, who modifies the clothes. It is common for new models to try to adjust the clothes themselves, which can be annoying if they are in a perfect position or if it has taken time to help them master a pose.

Standing behind the photographer allows you to see what he or she sees. If the photographer notices a problem with the clothes and asks you to amend them, you will know instantly what he is referring to because your positioning and eye line will be the same as his. Standing behind also means you won't get in the photographer's way or in the shot! If you need to enter the set to alter the clothes then say so and the photographer will wait until you have finished before shooting again. Occasionally a styling idea may not work as you have envisaged it, so move on and try another idea and something more interesting may take its place; remember that this is a test shoot, which is designed to test your styling ideas.

As the shoot progresses the photographer should keep a selection of the best shots on a laptop so the team can see the story developing. The looks prepared towards the end of the day might change a little as you react to the first combination of shots. For example, if you have lots of good full-length shots the team may decide to focus on a close-up shot of the model's head and shoulders. This may change what you have planned for the remaining photographs. A head shot will exclude clothes and shoes being worn on the model's lower half and you may want to add jewellery, a collar or hat or rethink the make-up and hair as it now forms a prominent part of the image.

○ **Behind the scenes of a fashion shoot on location.**
Styling by Charlotte Lightfoot
Photography: Kelly Cochrane

Clothing care

The clothes are solely the responsibility of the stylist; taking care of them is your job before, during and after the shoot. Keep clothes organized and tidy as you work. If you have an assistant make sure that they pack away things that aren't needed; putting clothes back on original hangers, shoes in boxes and repackaging items with tissue or tags. Managing the clothing in this way means that there will be less to do when the shoot is finished. This could be critical if you have a narrow window in which to shoot, pack up and leave a location.

When the shoot is over any borrowed clothes should be returned in their original packaging, ideally the following day. It is extremely bad practice to hold on to clothes and if you do this it will jeopardize your ability to borrow from the same source again. Make a list of the items being returned, when and by whom.

Working to your test brief

With so many creative minds involved in one shoot it is entirely plausible that the team gets carried away with things, spending too long on one shot. Try to stick to the test brief and refer to the call sheet to move the process on. Always try to work to the number of photos you need and if you have time at the end of the day you can experiment further. Finally, keep to the agreed times when working at a studio or location space; on a professional shoot you would certainly be charged for going over your allotted time.

○ Testing editorial ideas using projections.
Photography: Moira Sprunt and Adam Beazley

Post-production techniques involve enhancing and transforming images using software such as Adobe Photoshop. As with the picture editing process, the photographer is usually responsible for digitally manipulating the photographs although stylists and most art and design students have a good grasp of the software; you may be taught photo-editing as part of your course. Manipulation of photographs can take numerous forms. There are endless possibilities when considering digital editing techniques. The model can be removed from the original location and dropped into another scene, their hair and eye colour can be changed or a photograph converted into an illustration. If the photographer is assigned to edit the test shoot images the team can discuss what type of editing, and how much, is best for the story.

◐ ◑ Colour variations applied during the post-production process.
Styling: Andrea Billing
Photography: Adam Beazley

Photo manipulation and retouching

It is possible to alter the whole image in a basic way by varying brightness, changing the contrast of light and dark and de-saturating it (removing colour, which converts it to black and white). Images will then be 'cleaned up' by removing imperfections such as marks on the backdrop paper or the stylist's hand in the shot. At this point the model's hair and skin can be cleverly corrected by removing spots; dark circles under the eyes that still show through the make-up or a stray hair across the face.

◑ ◐ **Experimenting with post-production ideas.**
Styling: Claire Johnson
Photography: Laura E Oliver

◐ Collage layout: image repeated, torn and laid over the other.
Styling: Kate Geaney
Photography: Lindsay Jill-Cox

◐ Artwork by Patrick Waugh for studioBOYO.
Photography: Alasdair McLellan
Styling: Jane Howe

Layout

Photographs can often be the start of the creative process rather than the end. The layout stage of the process provides you with an opportunity to practise your creative technique. Experiment with straightforward or creative crops; repeat or collage the images, both digitally and by hand. Design a fashion editorial by cropping and formatting the images into a fashion magazine layout, with a title, text and graphics. Arrange the images to resemble a lookbook, complete with clothing descriptions; or a promotional advertisement with fashion logo. Alternatively, it is perfectly acceptable for photographs to be printed and simply displayed in a portfolio without any special layouts. Taking into account personal preferences, image layout may be approached quite differently by the stylist, photographer and the make-up artist.

In 2009 online fashion retail sales amounted to over £17 billion in the UK. Womenswear and menswear sales were second only to books and CDs as the most purchased products on the Internet. Fashion customers need to be able to view products quickly and clearly so the navigation must be simple, with consideration given to the product details. Look on most fashion retail sites and you will see a high volume of products and images; there are often thousands of products at any one time and the e-tailer will possibly introduce thousands more products each week. Commercial styling for the printed page and for the Internet is largely the same: both require the same set of techniques and skills. However, the number of products and the speed at which they are continually uploaded means that, in order to meet the demand, stylists have to work extremely quickly and accurately.

↻ ↺ Mini film clips of models wearing clothing on the runway for ASOS.

Animation and interaction

It is important for consumers to have the closest view of a product possible. Details such as colour, fabric and texture, trims and details have to be as clear as web technology will allow. The most common facilities on websites today grant shoppers the ability to zoom and rotate the product using a mouse. This technique is particularly used in product-only shots, such as footwear, where the different silhouette views and heel height can play an important part in the buying decision. This method usually requires a photograph of the front and back, and possibly a side view, as well as close-up shots that highlight a print, for example, or embellished detail.

Stop motion animation is used to create a complete 360-degree view, or more detailed view, of a product. This technique involves taking a series of individual shots; when the images are played in sequence, the product appears to move. This is a creative way of styling a product that has an interesting detail, such as a handbag opening to reveal a contrasting lining.

Most fashion websites illustrate the silhouette and fit of a garment by presenting it on a mannequin or real model. This method has become standard in fashion e-tailing. Film clips are also being used successfully by e-tailers, which give customers access to the 'exclusivity' of a catwalk show as each clip is accompanied by a cool soundtrack.

Styling for the Internet > Online blogs and magazines

Online magazines

Most print publications now have associated websites, which offer projects that print cannot accommodate, such as sound and moving image. Internet publications in this instance can show an interview, fashion advertisement or music video. At present, digital and print publications are sitting happily alongside each other – *Dazed & Confused* runs Dazed Digital; *Love* magazine has an iTunes application for iPad – but it is uncertain how the digital versus print debate will evolve. Will the immediacy of the online world challenge the longer lead times involved in publishing monthly, quarterly or bi-annual magazines?

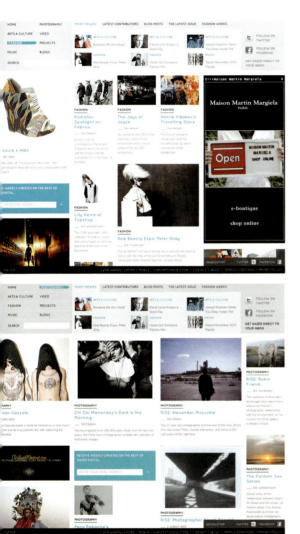

Blogs

The Internet has also given rise to the boom in self-publishing. Blogs (web-logs) enable everyone to express an opinion about fashion. Bloggers are often central to their own writing and use their blog as a diary to highlight their own interests and research; to illustrate their personal sense of style, by uploading images of themselves; and to interact with other like-minded bloggers within a community. Starting a blog is a great way for you to research and reflect on fashion and to practise your writing skills. Fashion blogs have become a great research tool: their accessible nature means that fashion designers and stylists can easily tap into what younger people are discussing, reading, buying and listening to around the world. Amateur bloggers with large followings have also found their way into the events usually reserved for more mainstream fashion journalists. Bloggers such as Susanna Lau (stylebubble.typepad.com) and Tavi Gevinson (thestylerookie.com) can be found in the front rows at international shows alongside the more established fashion press.

⊙ ◑ **Style bloggers Susanna Lau (stylebubble) and Sabrina Meijer (afterdrk).**

◑ **Dazed Digital is the online version of *Dazed and Confused* magazine.**

Catwalk shows and events offer great opportunities for stylists to employ their creativity and talent, whether they are a high-production event for a major designer, a retail fashion event for a shopping centre or a small-scale, low-budget show at college. Catwalk shows are still popular because the audience witnesses fashion theatre; seeing the clothes move, how fabric and colours react to lights.

Different types of shows obviously have very different audiences. Shows for press and buyers, such as those at New York Fashion Week, will be used to create as much exposure for the designer as possible and coverage of these shows will spread globally in newspapers and websites. The collections will influence fashion designers at the middle and lower end of the market, and, for fashion buyers, the shows will provide the first glimpse of the season's trends in which they will be investing.

Retail shows happen close to the season and are produced to show the buying public the ranges and trends that are available in-store and how to wear them. These shows work particularly well in large shopping malls where selections of shops provide the clothing. Charity catwalk shows are predominantly used as fundraising opportunities and also act as a promotional tool for the designers or retailers involved.

○ (Top) Backstage at William Tempest S/S11.
Catwalking.com

○ Backstage at Richard Nicoll A/W10 and S/S11.
Photography: Justine Grist

Fashion in motion

Fashion events

In addition to catwalk shows, stylists are often required to work on fashion-related events such as parties, store openings, press days and launch events for fashion ranges, perfumes, cosmetics and so on. These events are often held in retail stores, at a bar or club or at a specialist hired venue. Stylists may be employed to display a clothing or beauty range or to style the space. For press launches with a large number of fashion products, such as a mail-order company that sells many different sub-ranges, stylists may be brought in to edit the ranges into smaller, cohesive, trend-led stories. By editing ranges in this way, press visitors, such as fashion editors, can clearly see how these clothes fit into their fashion editorials.

'You have to get into the designer's mindset. You are there for them 24/7. So much time, love and care goes into it.'
Sophia Neophitou.

Producing a show

A catwalk show is a division of labour and it often requires a show producer to coordinate what happens before and during the event. However, depending on the scale of the show, a stylist may have a greater involvement than making the clothing look good on the runway; decisions have to be made on lighting, choreography and music.

Fashion garments worn on the catwalk will be viewed from all angles; therefore, the main responsibility of the stylist is to ensure the clothes fit the model as perfectly as possible. The clamps and pins used to adapt garments for a print shoot are clearly not acceptable at a show. Fashion on the catwalk is part of a live performance; it has to make an impact, engage the audience and hold their attention. Dramatic clothes with strong silhouettes often work well.

There is usually a terrific backstage buzz at a catwalk show but as the models glide out on to the runway the craziness of backstage dissipates, and the audience will expect to see a smooth, professionally organized show. If styling catwalk shows appeals to you it is wise to start backstage as a dresser, where you will witness the excitement, and chaos, behind the scenes. Learning how to dress a model within a given timeframe gives budding stylists vital insider information on the styling techniques that will or will not work. At smaller shows, where changeovers are fast and models have to get back to the catwalk quickly, it is not always possible to change items such as hosiery or gloves so styling ideas have to be adapted. Likewise, complicated outfits need to go on the runway first to avoid delays.

⊙ Backstage at the Ellery A/W10 show.
Photography: Cameron Smith

⊙ Backstage at the Emilio de la Morina S/S11 show.
Catwalking.com

Online blogs and magazines > **Catwalk shows and events** > Fashion film

Never before has the fashion buying public had so much access to 'insider' fashion information. It is now possible for everyone to see the collections from London Fashion Week streamed online 'as it happens' or to glimpse behind the scenes of a French *Vogue* shoot on YouTube.

In 2010 Burberry presented its S/S11 collection to invited customers at Burberry stores around the world. Rather than hold simultaneous catwalk shows in different locations Burberry played a film of their traditional fashion show and customers could order the looks straight from the catwalk. The shift to moving image in fashion has gathered pace and in the new millennium it is fashion film that has caught the imagination of designers and image makers alike. Nick Knight's website SHOWStudio has forged the way in this field. It has broadcast live from behind the scenes at photoshoots and fashion shows as well as collaborating with leading designers, models and stylists on a variety of multimedia projects. Gareth Pugh's A/W10 collection was filmed by Ruth Hogben and broadcast by SHOWStudio to buyers and journalists in Paris, replacing the traditional catwalk show. Other designers and fashion brands are increasingly experimenting with film; as with printed media, fashion film has not replaced the live show – yet.

○ Alexander McQueen integrated film into his S/S10 show. A digital film by Nick Knight, featuring Raquel Zimmerman, was presented on an 18-metre (60-foot) LED screen behind the catwalk and the show was broadcast to the world via twin robotic cameras and a link up with SHOWstudio.
Catwalking.com

'[There] were certain things that I believed in when we started SHOWStudio. One was process, the second was performance and the third was moving fashion.'
Nick Knight

**Clare Potts writes a style blog:
iliketweet.blogspot.com**

Whatever is happening during the day, I always make sure there is a blog post ready and waiting for the day ahead, which I usually publish at 7am. There's no reason behind me posting every day apart from the fact that I love it. My blog posts always have to be about something I love, whether that is beautiful photographs I've found in the recesses of the Internet or the work of a graduate from the other side of the world. After publishing the blog post for the day, I sort through my emails and reply to all the comments that have been left on my blog; this is great for me as I love to read other people's blogs too. I also make sure that I post about it on Twitter (@iliketweet) to make sure those readers that follow me on there will be able to read it too.

I post a lot of interviews with new designers and creatives on my blog, so it's important for me to develop relationships, network and always be friendly, whether it be on the Internet or in 'real life'. I usually go to a couple of events per week, which are generally held in retail stores or at a popular venue, making the perfect conditions for viewing the product and having a chat to the people behind the brand. At events, I spend my time writing quotes, making connections and taking far too many photos. It is also great to meet other bloggers in the flesh; the former threat of meeting someone from the Internet is completely gone, and people who willingly splash their face all over their blog are rarely retiring wallflowers.

As a blogger, you need to be on top of the trends coming up for the next season but you also need to keep your own personal style, as that is why people will keep reading a blog. I make sure to show my face every now and then, but I generally prefer to post about new designers and photographers that my readers may not have heard of before.

My day usually ends with me preparing a blog post for the next day, whether this is completing a whole post or just finding images. I enjoy the blogging process so it's a nice way to wind down after a full day.

tweet

fashion, photography, art and ellipsis...

TUESDAY, 9 NOVEMBER 2010

Takumi Yanazaki

ebay

email

twitter

bloglovin

jfb

chictopia

Unfathomable Depths

Tic Stars
lipstickkk
Little Miss Dress Up
LIVE GLAMOUR DIE
LONDON ROSE
Love from Lou Lou
Lovenlogs
Mademoiselle Robot
Magpie girl
Manchester Fashion Network
MANIKU
meeka see whippee
Muriel's Castle
Nearly Thirty
Neater This
NICE TRY, RADIO
Not Fashionista, Calling Stylista
Not So Prim and Proper
NQFires
Oh, cuttsey this crack on
Old School Cool
Orchid Grey
Pink Beaune
POLKA DOTS
Pretty Much Penniless
Pretty Particlulle
Princess Dominique
PSYNIPADS
RAGS
Ramblee
Ring My Bell
Rings, Save a banana!
Ripped Velon
Rosenfelt & Dreinkleyds

chictopia

facebook

features

The Connected Consoles
Dina Sherman
Shop It To Me Fashionista
Sketchbook Play
Style Bubble Musings
Unfathomable Depths
Ring My Bell

CHAU MAR LEE

about

You are more than welcome to use the images shown on my blog as long as you link back to the original post and credit them.

If you're interested in exchanging links, featuring your brand on my blog or advertising just email me at clarecotts@googlemail.com.

I am a Chictopia ambassador. Click here for my personal invite.

Jana Kossaibati

Jana Kossaibati writes a blog for fashion-conscious Muslim women: www.hijabstyle.co.uk

I started blogging in September 2007, having found little in the way of magazines or websites that focused on Muslim women's clothing needs. It began with posting high-street finds or outfits, links to Islamic clothing companies and a few random articles I could find online. I didn't really go in with a clear idea of what I wanted the blog to look like, or how I could develop it. But over time and as I got to grips with blogging, I realized that there really was a demand for somewhere Muslim women could turn to for help with dressing modestly, whilst maintaining their own personal sense of style.

As a medical student, a typical day for me revolves around my university schedule, and time for blogging needs to fit around this. Being organized is essential, so I'll usually have a few posts ready in advance, and they can be scheduled to post in the morning. It is at times difficult to keep motivated and post new content, especially during exam time. However, covering Islamic fashion around the world means that content is quite varied – everything from outfits, designer interviews, street style, news, runway fashion coverage and readers' contributions. This means that there is usually a constant stream of new topics to cover and write about.

When it comes to the content of the blog posts, there are a lot of resources I use depending on what I'm going to be writing. If it's a post about modest runway fashions, I'll use Style.com. Google news keeps me updated with the latest hijab and Islamic fashion articles, and often companies will email me to let me know about new collections, events, offers and so on. Increasingly, however, a lot of my time is spent doing 'backstage' work, rather than directly working on blog posts. This includes doing media interviews, contributing articles, responding to a large number of emails and maintaining social network pages for my blog, namely Facebook and Twitter. This does take away from the time I can spend on blog content; however, it does mean the influence that Hijab Style has is far greater than just the blog on its own.

Even though my education is in a totally different field, being constantly busy in itself motivates me to keep on top of things and stay organized. I also like the fact that my interests are not restricted to academia; the blog provides a welcome relief from studies and has helped me meet and work with a larger variety of people.

www.hijabstyle.co.uk

hijabstyle.blogspot.com

Interview: Clare Potts > Interview: Jana Kossaibati > Interview: Matthew Pike

Matthew Pike

Fashion promotion student Matthew Pike writes a men's fashion blog: buckets-and-spades.blogspot.com

The motivation for starting up my blog was purely to create a place where I could store all my ideas and pictures, which were gathering on my computer; another big factor was that I really wanted to improve my writing skills. These two factors are still relevant three years down the line. The other main motivation is that I have quite loyal readers and I feel like I have entered into a close-knit community and there is a certain buzz around everybody reading everyone else's blogs. Basically you start to build up online friendships, but this spans further to online social networks, like Facebook and Twitter. I also write to keep myself busy; people seem to like what I have to say/post and lots of great opportunities have come my way over the past few years.

I have run two competitions on my blog; the recent one not only helped build a professional relationship with the company (I am in talks for another one and an interview for my blog) but also granted me lots of new followers and traffic. Both times the companies approached me; again, social networks have a massive role to play, especially when you can directly talk to any company you like.

When it comes down to it, I am just a blogger and since blogging has become big news a lot of people have abused it and tried to get as much out of it as possible. This is fine when it comes to going to press events and getting tickets here and there but when people start to write about stuff in the hope they get a freebie, I think you have to tread carefully. You really have to look at what you want out of it: if it's a stepping stone, which leads to something greater, or if you just want to become the next z-lister. Integrity is key. One of my favourite blogs has always been Style Salvage – written by a male and female about men's style; not so much 'fashion'. You will find most menswear blogs concentrate on style over fashion: timeless qualities over trend-led. I think this is what makes menswear restricting but exciting.

buckets & spades

the life of a boy who lives by the seaside

home • about • links • twitter • email

8.11.10
Freunde von Freunden's Interviews

BUCKETS

AWARDS

Fashion 100

CURRENT FAVS
Dapper Kid
Hapsical
Jazzabelle's Diary
Lineage of Influence
Lipstick & Balloons
milk
Not Just Medical
Style Salvage
Stylenest
Things Organized Neatly

CURRENTLY LIKING
-'An Idiot Abroad'
-'Wallpaper' magazine
-American workwear
-DJ
-Beige Converse
-Arcade Fire & C. W Stoneking
-Sciencey stuff

buckets & spades

the life of a boy who lives by the seaside

home • about • links • twitter • email

30.11.10
Snow Days

Mirror Image

► November (7)
► October (10)
► September (10)
► August (8)
► July (13)
► June (10)
► May (10)
► April (15)
► March (17)
► February (22)
► January (13)
► 2009 (180)
► 2008 (42)

FOLLOWERS

Follow
with Google Friend Connect
Followers (225)   More »

Already a member? Sign in

tollsweep

LN·CC
URBAN OUTFITTERS EUROPE
COGGLES.COM
my
All I want for Christmas...
► SHOP NOW

Arnold, Rebecca
American Look: Fashion and the Image of Women in 1930s and 1940s New York
IB Tauris (2008)

Barnard, Malcolm
Fashion as Communication
Routledge (1996)

Baudot, François
Chanel
Editions Assouline (2004)

Baxter-Wright, Emma; Clarkson, Karen; Kennedy, Sarah and Mulvey, Kate
Vintage Fashion
Carlton Books (2010)

Calasibetta, Charlotte Mankey; Tortora, Phyllis G and Abling, Bina
Fairchild Dictionary of Fashion
Fairchild Books (2003)

Carter, Graydon and Foley, Bridget
Tom Ford: Ten Years
Thames & Hudson (2004)

Cotton, Charlotte
Imperfect Beauty: The Making of Contemporary Fashion Photographs
V & A Publications (2000)

Derrick, Robin and Muir, Robin
Unseen Vogue: The Secret History of Fashion Photography
Little, Brown & Company (2004)

Derrick, Robin and Muir, Robin
Vogue Covers: On Fashion's Front Page
Little, Brown (2009)

Diane, Tracey and Cassidy, Tom
Colour Forecasting
John Wiley & Sons (2005)

Dwight, Eleanor
Diana Vreeland
HarperCollins (2002)

Fukai, Akiko; Suoh, Tamami; Iwagami, Miki; Koga, Reiko; and Nie, Rii
Fashion: A History from the 18th to the 20th Century
Taschen (2006)

Jackson, Tim and Shaw, David
The Fashion Handbook
Routledge (2006)

Jaeger, Anne-Celine
Fashion Makers Fashion Shapers
Thames & Hudson (2009)

Jeffrey, Ian
The Photo Book
Phaidon (2005)

Jobling, Paul
Fashion Spreads: Word and Image in Fashion Photography since 1980
Berg (1999)

Jones, Terry
Smile i-D: Fashion and Style: the Best from 20 Years of i-D
Taschen (2001)

Jones, Terry and Rushton, Susie
Fashion Now 2
Taschen (2005)

Keaney, Magdalene
Fashion and Advertising
RotoVision (2007)

Koda, Harold
Extreme Beauty: The Body Transformed
Yale University Press (2001)

Koda, Harold
Model as Muse
Yale University Press (2009)

Lagerfeld, Karl and Harlech, Amanda
Visions and a Decision
Steidl (2007)

Mackrell, Alice
Art and Fashion
Batsford (2005)

Martin, Penny
When You're a Boy: Men's fashion styled by Simon Foxton
Photographers' Gallery (2009)

Martin, Richard; Mackrell, Alice; Rickey, Melanie and Buttolph, Angela
The Fashion Book
Phaidon (2001)

Maxwell, Kim
Career Diary of a Fashion Stylist: Thirty Days Behind the Scenes With a Professional
Garth Gardner Company (2007)

Morgan, Jamie and Lorenz, Mitzi
Buffalo: The Style and Fashion of Ray Petri
powerHouse Books (2000)

Mower, Sarah
Stylist: The Interpreters of Fashion
Rizzoli International Publications (2007)

Müller, Florence
Art & Fashion
Thames & Hudson (2000)

Roberts, Michael
Grace: Thirty Years of Fashion at Vogue
Steidl Verlag (2002)

Scheips, Charles
American Fashion: Council of Fashion Designers of America
Assouline (2007)

Schuman, Scott
The Sartorialist
Penguin (2009)

Shinkle, Eugenie
Fashion as Photograph: Viewing and Reviewing Images of Fashion
IB Tauris (2008)

Squiers, Carol; Aletti, Vincent; Garner, Phillippe and Hartshorn, Willis
Avedon Fashion 1944–2000
Harry N. Abrams (2009)

Tungate, Mark
Fashion Brands: Branding Style from Armani to Zara
Kogan Page (2008)

Walford, Jonathan
Forties Fashion: From Siren Suits to the New Look
Thames & Hudson (2008)

Walker, Tim
Pictures
teNeues (2008)

Watson, Linda
Vogue Fashion
Carlton Books (2008)

Weil, Christa
It's Vintage, Darling! How to be a Clothes Connoisseur
Hodder & Stoughton (2006)

Stylists' agencies

Katie Grand: www.clmuk.com

Katy England: www.smiletoo.com

Nicola Forminchetti: www.clmuk.com

Simon Foxton: www.clmuk.com

Contributor websites

www.adrianmesko.com

www.alexanderlockett.co.uk

www.antonz.com.au

www.cameronsmithphoto.com

www.christophershannon.co.uk

www.clarebuckley.com

www.elleryland.com

www.ellie-noble.co.uk

www.emmajadeparker.co.uk

www.feaverishphotography.com/
blog/2010/06/akila-berjaoui/

www.hollyblake.net

www.iprlondon.com

www.jamiehawkesworth.com

www.jonasbresnan.com

www.milosmali.com

www.mrjames.co.uk

www.mvetolskiy.blogspot.com

www.richardnicoll.com

www.scotttrindle.com

www.studioboyo.com

www.willdavidson.com

General websites and blogs

www.artsthread.com

www.colinmcdowell.com

www.fashioninfilm.com

www.fashiontoast.com

www.gfw.org.uk

www.lookbook.nu

www.magculture.com/blog

www.models.com

www.rdfranks.co.uk

www.showstudio.com

www.style.com

www.stylebubble.typepad.com

www.thesartorialist.blogspot.com

www.thestylerookie.com

www.theurbangent.com

Fashion trade shows

www.londonfashionweek.co.uk

www.moda-uk.co.uk

www.modeaparis.com

www.pretparis.com

www.purelondon.com

Galleries and museums

Fashion and Textiles Museum, UK
www.ftmlondon.org

Fashion Museum, UK
www.museumofcostume.co.uk

Jeu de Paume, Paris
www.jeudepaume.org

Metropolitan Museum of Art, New York
www.metmuseum.org

Musée des Arts décoratif, Paris
www.lesartsdecoratifs.fr

Museum of Modern Art, New York
www.moma.org

The Photographers' Gallery
www.photonet.org.uk

Tate, UK
www.tate.org.uk

Victoria and Albert Museum, UK
www.vam.ac.uk

Acknowledgements

We would like to thank the following for their support and generous contributions:

Coco @ http://cocopit.biz/tag/illustrator, Tim Walker, Jacob K, Will Davidson, Christopher Shannon, Patrick Waugh, Richard Nicoll, Louise Goldin, Jonas Unger, Jamie Hawkesworth, Scott Trindle, Marcus Palmqvist, Milos Mali, Anton Zemlyanoy, Adrian Mesko, Jonas Bresnan, Kym Ellery, Debbie Cartwright, Graeme Black, Ezra Patchett, Justine Grist, *The Guardian* magazine, *Russh* magazine, Anthony Campbell, Katie Naunton-Morgan, Holly Blake, Ruzenka @ rp represents, Anna Hustler @ M.A.P London, Marsha Vetolskiy, Akila Berjaoui, Cameron Smith, Dave Schofield, Alexander Lockett, James Naylor, Alex Hurst, Chloe Amer, Emma Jade Parker, Carol Woollam, Jana Kossaibati, Siobhan Lyons, Clare Potts, Matt Pike, Francesca Middleton, Charlotte Lightfoot and our colleagues Professor Lubaina Himid MBE, Melanie Charman, Amanda Odlin-Bates and Steve Terry.

Our appreciation also extends to the staff, students and graduates of UCLan, along with the many stylists, photographers, models and hair and make-up artists who continue to give their valuable input and expertise on styling projects.

Special gratitude goes to Fashion Promotion with Styling graduates Andrea Billing and Kate Geaney for their continuous assistance in compiling this publication.

We would like to offer our sincere thanks to our editor Rachel Netherwood for her support and guidance throughout the project. Thank you to Pseudonym for the design.

Finally, to our families, Peter and Sally Buckley, Sarah Buckley, Margaret and Denis McAssey and Damien Doyle and to our friends; how could we have done this without your endless encouragement and patience.

Index

Picture credits

Cover courtesy and copyright of Coco

p 004 (left) photography by Jonas Bresnan; (middle) collage by Patrick Waugh for StudioBOYO, photography by Scott Trindle, styling by Sebastian Clivaz for *Wallpaper* magazine; (right) photography by Akila Berjaoui, styling by Leticia Dare for www.fashiongonerogue.com

p 005 (left) photography by Marcus Palmqvist for Jojo and Malou; (middle) photography by Will Davidson, styling by Clare Richardson for V Man; (right) photography by Milos Mali, styling by Clare Buckley for *Russh* magazine

p 059 photography by Andy Croasdale

p 062 courtesy and copyright of Paramount / The Kobal Collection

p 063 courtesy and copyright of MGM / The Kobal Collection

p 092 (right) layout designed by Melanie Charman

p 100 courtesy and copyright of NBCU Photobank / Rex Features

pp 106–109 courtesy of Emma Jade Parker

pp 110–111 courtesy of Alex Hurst

p 172 courtesy of Esther Coenen

pp 180–181 photography by Will Epps

All reasonable attempts have been made to trace, clear and credit the copyright holders of the images reproduced in this book. However, if any credits have been inadvertently omitted, the publisher will endeavour to incorporate amendments in future editions.

Publisher's note

The subject of ethics is not new, yet its consideration within the applied visual arts is perhaps not as prevalent as it might be. Our aim here is to help a new generation of students, educators and practitioners find a methodology for structuring their thoughts and reflections in this vital area.

AVA Publishing hopes that these **Working with ethics** pages provide a platform for consideration and a flexible method for incorporating ethical concerns in the work of educators, students and professionals. Our approach consists of four parts:

The **introduction** is intended to be an accessible snapshot of the ethical landscape, both in terms of historical development and current dominant themes.

The **framework** positions ethical consideration into four areas and poses questions about the practical implications that might occur. Marking your response to each of these questions on the scale shown will allow your reactions to be further explored by comparison.

The **case study** sets out a real project and then poses some ethical questions for further consideration. This is a focus point for a debate rather than a critical analysis so there are no predetermined right or wrong answers.

A selection of **further reading** for you to consider areas of particular interest in more detail.

Ethical: aware-
ness/
reflect-
ion/
debate

Working with ethics

Introduction

Ethics is a complex subject that interlaces the idea of responsibilities to society with a wide range of considerations relevant to the character and happiness of the individual. It concerns virtues of compassion, loyalty and strength, but also of confidence, imagination, humour and optimism. As introduced in ancient Greek philosophy, the fundamental ethical question is: *what should I do?* How we might pursue a 'good' life not only raises moral concerns about the effects of our actions on others, but also personal concerns about our own integrity.

In modern times the most important and controversial questions in ethics have been the moral ones. With growing populations and improvements in mobility and communications, it is not surprising that considerations about how to structure our lives together on the planet should come to the forefront. For visual artists and communicators, it should be no surprise that these considerations will enter into the creative process.

Some ethical considerations are already enshrined in government laws and regulations or in professional codes of conduct. For example, plagiarism and breaches of confidentiality can be punishable offences. Legislation in various nations makes it unlawful to exclude people with disabilities from accessing information or spaces. The trade of ivory as a material has been banned in many countries. In these cases, a clear line has been drawn under what is unacceptable.

But most ethical matters remain open to debate, among experts and lay-people alike, and in the end we have to make our own choices on the basis of our own guiding principles or values. Is it more ethical to work for a charity than for a commercial company? Is it unethical to create something that others find ugly or offensive?

Specific questions such as these may lead to other questions that are more abstract. For example, is it only effects on humans (and what they care about) that are important, or might effects on the natural world require attention too?

Is promoting ethical consequences justified even when it requires ethical sacrifices along the way? Must there be a single unifying theory of ethics (such as the Utilitarian thesis that the right course of action is always the one that leads to the greatest happiness of the greatest number), or might there always be many different ethical values that pull a person in various directions?

As we enter into ethical debate and engage with these dilemmas on a personal and professional level, we may change our views or change our view of others. The real test though is whether, as we reflect on these matters, we change the way we act as well as the way we think. Socrates, the 'father' of philosophy, proposed that people will naturally do 'good' if they know what is right. But this point might only lead us to yet another question: *how do we know what is right?*

Working with ethics

You
What are your ethical beliefs?

Central to everything you do will be your attitude to people and issues around you. For some people, their ethics are an active part of the decisions they make every day as a consumer, a voter or a working professional. Others may think about ethics very little and yet this does not automatically make them unethical. Personal beliefs, lifestyle, politics, nationality, religion, gender, class or education can all influence your ethical viewpoint.

Using the scale, where would you place yourself? What do you take into account to make your decision? Compare results with your friends or colleagues.

Your client
What are your terms?

Working relationships are central to whether ethics can be embedded into a project, and your conduct on a day-to-day basis is a demonstration of your professional ethics. The decision with the biggest impact is whom you choose to work with in the first place. Cigarette companies or arms traders are often-cited examples when talking about where a line might be drawn, but rarely are real situations so extreme. At what point might you turn down a project on ethical grounds and how much does the reality of having to earn a living affect your ability to choose?

Using the scale, where would you place a project? How does this compare to your personal ethical level?

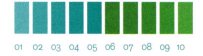

01 02 03 04 05 06 07 08 09 10

01 02 03 04 05 06 07 08 09 10

Your specifications
What are the impacts of your materials?

In relatively recent times, we are learning that many natural materials are in short supply. At the same time, we are increasingly aware that some man-made materials can have harmful, long-term effects on people or the planet. How much do you know about the materials that you use? Do you know where they come from, how far they travel and under what conditions they are obtained? When your creation is no longer needed, will it be easy and safe to recycle? Will it disappear without a trace? Are these considerations your responsibility or are they out of your hands?

Using the scale, mark how ethical your material choices are.

Your creation
What is the purpose of your work?

Between you, your colleagues and an agreed brief, what will your creation achieve? What purpose will it have in society and will it make a positive contribution? Should your work result in more than commercial success or industry awards? Might your creation help save lives, educate, protect or inspire? Form and function are two established aspects of judging a creation, but there is little consensus on the obligations of visual artists and communicators toward society, or the role they might have in solving social or environmental problems. If you want recognition for being the creator, how responsible are you for what you create and where might that responsibility end?

Using the scale, mark how ethical the purpose of your work is.

Working with ethics

01 02 03 04 05 06 07 08 09 10

01 02 03 04 05 06 07 08 09 10

One aspect of fashion design that raises an ethical dilemma is the way that clothes production has changed in terms of the speed of delivery of products and the now international chain of suppliers. 'Fast fashion' gives shoppers the latest styles sometimes just weeks after they first appeared on the catwalk, at prices that mean they can wear an outfit once or twice and then replace it. Due to lower labour costs in poorer countries, the vast majority of Western clothes are made in Asia, Africa, South America or Eastern Europe in potentially hostile and sometimes inhumane working conditions. It can be common for one piece of clothing to be made up of components from five or more countries, often thousands of miles apart, before they end up in the high-street store. How much responsibility should a fashion designer have in this situation if manufacture is controlled by retailers and demand is driven by consumers? Even if designers wish to minimise the social impact of fashion, what might they most usefully do?

Traditional Hawaiian feather capes (called *'Ahu'ula*) were made from thousands of tiny bird feathers and were an essential part of aristocratic regalia. Initially they were red (*'Ahu'ula* literally means 'red garment') but yellow feathers, being especially rare, became more highly prized and were introduced to the patterning.

The significance of the patterns, as well as their exact age or place of manufacture is largely unknown, despite great interest in their provenance in more recent times. Hawaii was visited in 1778 by English explorer Captain James Cook and feather capes were amongst the objects taken back to Britain.

The basic patterns are thought to reflect gods or ancestral spirits, family connections and an individual's rank or position in society. The base layer for these garments is a fibre net, with the surface made up of bundles of feathers tied to the net in overlapping rows. Red feathers came from the *'i'iwi* or the *'apapane*. Yellow feathers came from a black bird with yellow tufts under each wing called *'oo'oo*, or a *mamo* with yellow feathers above and below the tail.